For the Future of Norway

Little Norway

in Pictures

WITH SUPPLEMENT
NORWAY - YESTERDAY AND TODAY

S. J. Reginald Saunders
Publisher, Toronto

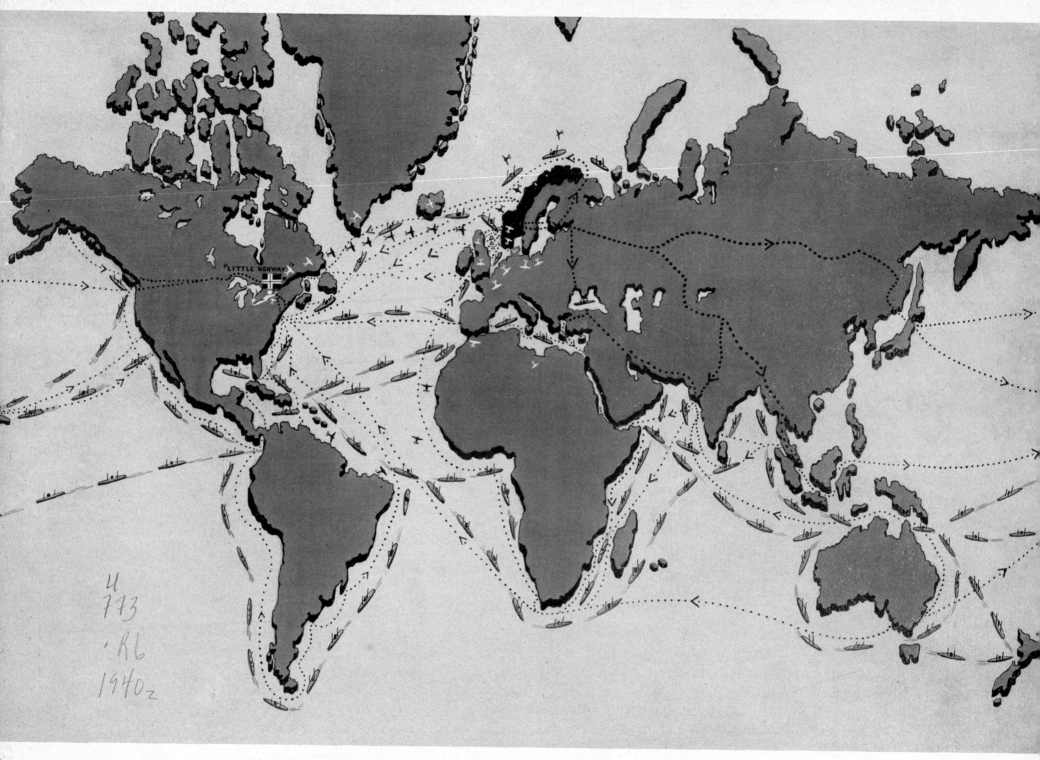

THE ROUTES OF NORWEGIAN VOLUNTEERS TO LITTLE NORWAY

Dotted lines show the travel routes.   The ships show the position of the fourth largest Merchant Marine in the world—Norway's greatest
contribution to this war.   Planes indicate spheres of Norwegian training, fighter, bomber and ferry command activities.

Norway — Yesterday and Today

IN THE FOOTSTEPS OF ERIC THE RED

Yes, but is it friend or foe—will he warn the navy or bomb us?

If, say in June, 1939, you had told Ola Myra that he would leave his home within two years, and go to Toronto, Canada . . . that he would leave his family, his friends and his Norway, escaping across the North Sea during the height of a bitter, mid-December gale . . . that he would sail across the Atlantic in daily danger of sudden death . . . that he would become a proud member of the daring Royal Norwegian Air Force . . . that, in the short space of two years, he would be transplanted from his picturesque Norwegian fjord to the shores of Lake Ontario . . . that he would be transformed from a peaceful, freedom-loving citizen to a determined, revenge-seeking army pilot . . . in fact, if you had even suggested as much, Ola would have said, "It just *can't* happen! *Det kan ikke hende!* It just *can't* happen!"

Perhaps Ola, as he sailed up the broad Gulf of St. Lawrence, perhaps as he first sighted the green bounds of Canada, he recaptured the spirit of *Leiv Erikson*, who, more than nine centuries before, had sailed these waters and first discovered this welcoming land.

Ola, following in the footsteps of Erik the Red, thrilled as the Norse blood of generations of daring seafarers coursed through his veins when he approached this new-found home, excited, in anticipation of the great adventure just ahead.

Past the familiar looking North Shore, rugged and tree-lined, through the quaint Habitant country of French Canada, with the blue Laurentians rising in the background, through cosmopolitan Montreal and on to friendly Toronto to a welcome worthy of the best that his homeland itself could offer, finally arriving at "Little Norway", his Canadian home.

Thus Ola, six foot and blond, just like thousands of other Norwegian boys, arrived to start the training that was to translate his hatred, his courage, his determination into the spirit, the action and the daring for which the Royal Norwegian Air Force is noted as it strikes back in ever-increasing strength, seeking revenge which only will be satisfied when the last bestial Nazi has been driven from Norway, that beautiful land which was so treacherously attacked and wickedly plundered.

No wonder Ola hated. No wonder he studied and trained with enthusiasm and diligence, anxious for the day when he could return to his native land and once again follow the pursuits of peace.

Ola was too modest to talk at length of his escape from Norway. Unpleasant memories made it difficult for him to relate the hardships of his fellow-countrymen under the Nazi heel — of threats, torture, reprisals, hostages, concentration camps — of lack of food, loss of weight, patched and tattered clothing, commandeered homes — of the Gestapo, and traitors . . . the whole unpleasant language of occupation, plunder, torture and death!

He preferred to refer to the Norwegian spirit and courage which remained undaunted, unconquered and steadfast in the very face of all the indignities heaped upon his people in the vain attempt to make them slaves. To him the triumph of truth and of the spirit was a source of pride which never failed to gain a warm response from his new-found Canadian and American friends.

If you asked Ola about "Little Norway", the training-ground of new-born Norway, he would be all enthusiasm, explaining about the schoolrooms, chart rooms, instrument rooms, Link trainers, radio apparatus, the modern equipment and planes, all of which were made possible by funds supplied by the Norwegian Merchant Marine and the brave Norwegian sailors risking their lives transporting supplies to the battlefronts of the United Nations in every corner of the globe. This complete training program which took him, a raw recruit, and in ten brief weeks passed him through Vesle Skaugum, the typically Norwegian recreation and recruiting centre created in the woods of Northern Ontario; then to the elementary flying school in Muskoka with its beautiful log cabins of Norwegian design planned by a former *Oslo* architect serving with the R.N.A.F.; on to R.A.F. and R.C.A.F. Schools throughout Canada to complete his training at the Island Airport in Toronto. Here, at the Island, he received advanced training with Curtiss Fighters or Douglas Bombers — real combat craft purchased by the Norwegian Government, in most cases prior to the German invasion but undelivered in Norway at that time.

To him "Little Norway" stands as a living symbol of something invincible which no force in this world can ever crush: a free man's spirit and a free man's will to fight for those principles which have proved to be dearer than life itself — the only lasting foundations of a peaceful, just and happy relationship between individuals and nations. As summed up in the words of General *Otto Ruge*, "No nation can rise again merely by waiting for something to happen, for some help to come from the outside. You must be ready to help yourself when the time is ripe. Wait, keep the faith, and be ready."

This spirit naturally received a warm response from Canadians and Americans alike, and aroused admiration in all parts of these two great countries.

But it was more than admiration even, or social formality, that opened the door for Ola to the Canadian hospitality which made this his "second home". It was his fair hair and blue eyes, his charming manner, and his eagerness to tell of his Norway — the Norway before the war — which made him such a welcome guest in the homes of Toronto, New York, Boston or Banff.

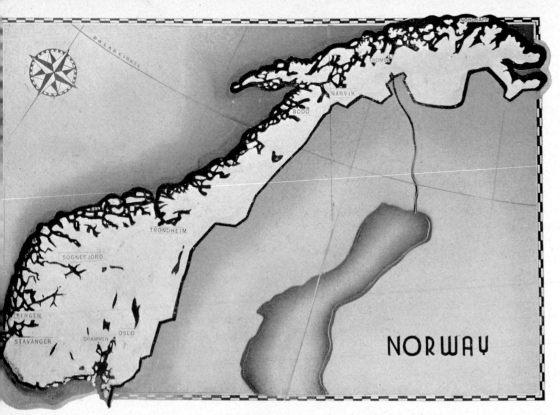

Norway's coastline of more than 25,000 miles in length is shown on this map.

accepting the universal principle of Christianity first introduced by King Olav the Holy. This turned the nation's life toward peaceful and constructive ventures.

NORWAY — COUNTRY OF THE FJORDS

It never took much prompting to start Ola talking about the beauty of his country. It was always difficult for him to stop, so much *had* to be told:

Norway is a long, narrow country, which, if turned around, using the Southern tip as a pivot, would stretch across Europe to the toe of Italy. If placed in the Western Hemisphere, Norway would stretch from Toronto to Trinidad and, at its widest point, from Chicago to Toronto.

Norway is a great plateau, which, in the beginning, was covered with an immense ice cap. During the ice age period, huge glaciers carved out the valleys and fjords and created what is today the famous island fringe *(skjaergaard)* forming protection for the inner channel and creating a beautiful cruise route and safe passage for coastwise shipping. Some of these islands, numbering more than 150,000 with a total area of 8,500 square miles, rise almost sheer from the water permitting vessels to pass at the very foot of towering cliffs, breath-taking at the very first glimpse — an impression never to be forgotten!

Famous throughout the world are the Norwegian fjords which line the coast forming a coastline of more than 25,000 miles, a distance greater than that around the world at the equator.

Those who have never visited Norway little realize the distance that many of these fjords penetrate into the country. Sogne Fjord, for example, runs for 136 miles into Norway, with a maximum depth of 670 fathoms. Surprising depth and precipitous cliffs rising abruptly from the water are characteristic of this typically Norwegian scenery the like of which is to be found nowhere else in the world.

Norangfjord, one of the thousand Norwegian fjords.

Almost in the manner of the sagas of old, those tales of early Norwegian life handed down from generation to generation by word of mouth, and recorded by the world-famous Saga writer Snorre Sturlaslon in his book called "Snorre Saga", Ola related the saga of Norway to his Canadian and American hosts.

THE LAND OF THE VIKINGS

A delightful dinner, chairs drawn close around a cosy fire usually inspired the saga of the Vikings:

In early times, the period from about 789 to 912 was known as the Viking Age of Norway, one of the most colorful and famous periods in Norwegian history, or, in fact, the history of the world. The Vikings, known as sea rovers, each Spring invaded England, Scotland, Ireland and Northern France. Beginning as desultory attacks they were followed by eventual settlements, inspiring in these other peoples a love of trade and sea-faring exploits.

The Viking boats were small and adapted to short voyages by sea in waters well studded with harbors. However, such was the courage of the Vikings, that many ventured upon distant and unknown waters in these ships ill fitted for the work. Under circumstances such as these, Leiv Erikson, Erik the Red, and a band of his hardy followers, boldly set foot on the shores of North America, calling the land Vinland, (Vineland). Love of native land, with the Vikings, as with the Norwegians of today inspired a desire to return quickly to their native land and thus this continent went practically unknown until "discovered" several hundred later years by Columbus.

The Viking period of Norway was the time for imperialistic expansion if such had been the ambition. Instead, the Norwegians outgrew the tendency of aggression, gradually

NORWAY'S CLIMATE IS KIND

Although Norway is chiefly in the same geographical position as that part of Canada lying above the Northern boundaries of Manitoba, Saskatchewan and Alberta, and roughly between the same latitudes as Alaska and the Yukon, the climate is comparatively mild along the West Coast. This is due to the Gulf Stream which visits Norway's shores with never-failing faithfulness. Along the West Coast, therefore, there is almost no snow in winter and the fjords remain ice-free.

Parts of the South-East country are rather flat with low, rolling hills and a climate similar to that in the Laurentians. Here we say that the people are "born on skis", in contrast to those of the West Coast who are "born in boats".

Along the Eastern boundary between Norway and Sweden lie hundreds of miles of deep forests. Dividing the country is a chain of mountains averaging about 7,000 feet. The snow line, which ranges from 3,080 feet to 5,150 feet, contributes to the grandeur of Norwegian mountains, and provides easily accessible year-round skiing.

PEOPLE OF NORWAY

As only about two and one-half per cent of the total area of Norway is suitable for agricultural purposes it is natural that the country has a limited population, which is considered generally to be around three million — about one-quarter the size of Metropolitan New York. In spite of this scarcity of population, there are about three million people of Norwegian descent in the United States. The closest relations of the Norwegians are the Icelanders, Swedes and Danes whose languages are similar. Throughout the centuries, the Norwegian strain has remained free of mixing, compared to that of most other nationalities. This is the reason for the typical Norwegian being tall, with blond hair and blue eyes. Perhaps the ruggedness of the country has tended to discourage immigration to Norway, although there has been some inter-marriage with the Scotch resulting in many common words and phrases.

The Norwegians are one of the most law-abiding people in the world. An absence of criminal tendencies makes the "Yearly Murder" always quite a sensation.

Oslo girls modeling ancient native costumes representing different districts in Norway.

From Left to Right:
Setersdalen, Numedal, Hallingdal.

Eidsvold Building the cradle of the Norwegian Constitution.

Little wonder that, when faced by *eighty million murderers*, these peace-loving Norwegians were at a decided disadvantage.

NORWEGIAN INDEPENDENCE

To Ola, May 17th was like July 1st to Canadians and July 4th to Americans — his chief National Festival or Holiday. May 17th commemorates the day, in 1814, when the Norwegian *Storting* (Parliament) assembled at Eidsvold, 40 miles north of *Oslo*, and declared Norway an independent kingdom. It was then that the most advanced democratic constitution known in Europe at that time was drawn up.

Those who framed this Constitution were able to benefit by the experience of the French and American constitutions. Instead of a President, a King symbolized the unity of the nation. A Cabinet, headed by a Prime Minister representing the strongest political party, carries out the will of the people. Invasion or earthquake, nothing can change the Norwegian constitution but a free Norwegian people. Slogan of the constitution, "*Enig og tro til Dovre faller*"(United and faithful till Dovre(mountains) fall) expresses the determination to maintain the freedom established at *Eidsvold*.

Back of the Norwegian *Storting* at *Eidsvold* lay many years of turmoil. For more than 400 years following the last of early Norse kings, King *Olav* in 1381, the country gradually became more and more under the control of Denmark, with a common king until about 1700, when it was almost reduced to the level of a Danish province.

With the defeat of Napoleon, Denmark, which had sided with him, lost Norway, which was ceded to Sweden by the Danish King. Norway rose in protest. A National Assembly was called which refused to acknowledge the treaty, declared Norway a free country, and drew up a New Constitution. War followed. This demonstration of its will to independence saved Norway from becoming a province of Sweden. Instead, Norway remained a "free, independent and indivisible kingdom united with Sweden under one King." Each country had its own parliament.

In 1821 the Storting passed a resolution creating the Norwegian Merchant flag — scarlet divided into four by a blue cross with white borders. In 1844 Norway had her own national flag with mark of the union with Sweden shown.

During the union with Sweden there was controversy between Sweden and Norway because the latter had no Foreign Minister and no opportunity to express its opinion in the field of foreign affairs. Eventually, on June 7, 1905, the Union was dissolved and Norway was declared a sovereign independent state.

Every male Norwegian citizen has the right and duty to serve in the Armed Forces when he reaches the age of twenty-one. Before the war, all branches of the Armed Services, the Army, the Navy and the Air Force, were partly modernized although their effectiveness was shattered by the unexpected, unprovoked, German sneak attack which made mobilization only partly possible. Nevertheless, the Norwegian forces under King *Haakon* fought on for sixty-two days and seriously upset Hitler's time-table by their unforeseen spirit against overwhelming odds.

Before the war Norway had eight political parties of which the Labour Party was almost equal in strength to all the others. The insignificant, so-called Nazi party was the smallest and without a single representative in either the parliament or local governments, giving some idea of how it was regarded by the people. Today, its numbers have decreased to one per cent of the population, leaving nothing but the utter dregs of the nation — the wicked and the weak.

Norway had some territories beyond its borders. Under the Versailles Treaty it administered Spitzbergen (*Svalbard*) by international agreement, in addition to the islands of *Jan Mayn*, *Björnnoya* and some Antarctic regions. A long-standing quarrel with Denmark over certain parts of Greenland was settled amicably by the International Court in the Hague in favour of Denmark without creating any national enmity.

NORWAY'S FAMOUS MERCHANT MARINE

Ola didn't have to tell much about the Merchant Marine. Canadians and Americans have read the story again and again, marvelling at its size and international importance. For it's a fact that Norway had the fourth largest Merchant Marine in the world in total tonnage — and the largest in the world when considered on a per capita basis.

The Norwegian Merchant Marine included the most modern Diesel tankers and floating whale-refineries in the world. Fast, modern vessels manned by men "born in boats" combine to make this service outstanding in every navigable water of the world, providing a yearly income of more than $200,000,-000.00, representing approximately 50% of the export of the nation.

Take whaling, for example.

Starting with specially-constructed small boats during the latter part of the Nineteenth Century, this industry has grown to great proportions with a world-wide production of one-and-one-half million barrels of oil yearly — a total catch equal to two-thirds of that of all other nations combined. Present-day, large floating refineries operate a pack of small whaling boats which hunt down the whales, shoot them, and tow them back to the mother ship for processing. Due to the scarcity of oils and fats the operation of these modern Norwegian whale oil refineries represents an important contribution to the cause of the United Nations.

Most of the ships managed to join the Allies and right now, about fifty per cent of Norway's Merchant Marine is intact, carrying supplies wherever the Allied war effort demands. In view of the heavy need for shipping and the losses suffered, this contribution has proved invaluable. Immobilized, or in the hands of the enemy, this would have made a great deal of difference in the progress of the war.

The *Oseberg* ship. Viking pleasure craft of the 9th century now preserved in museum near *Oslo*.

Three masted, full-rigged sailing vessel of the type which made the Norwegian Merchant Marine famous during the days of the sailing ship.

Modern liners such as *M.S. Oslofjord*, 18,673 tons gross, played a big part in Norway's place in the shipping world.

Stabur — a storehouse for food. The extended second floor increased the storage space and, being high off the ground, helped to protect the produce from rodents. This style is several centuries old.

hand, if a man from the West settles in the East, even if it is on a big stone, in two years he will have turned the stone into a little farm which will feed the cow and family. This shows the contrast in living conditions between the East and the West.

Co-operatives, which look after the common interests of the farmers, help to maintain and stabilize prices. This movement has been found successful in many other countries of the world.

The farmer holds a high position in the life of the nation. Quite often his father, grandfather, great-grandfather and his ancestors have lived and died on the same farm. This breeds a respect and reverence for the good earth which makes his farm a hallowed spot, not merely a business.

Ancient farm buildings in Norway dating back many centuries are now preserved as museums to show the role played by Norwegian farmers in the development of the Nation.

Ancient Norwegian ancestral home.

AGRICULTURE — BACKBONE OF NORWAY

Just as in Canada and the United States, so, too, in Norway Ola points out that farming is the true foundation of the country.

Agriculture is intensive. Up-to-date equipment and modern methods are typical. Cattle, in adequate quantity to meet the needs of the nation, are raised. Cheese, milk and vegetables are produced in sufficient quantity to provide an exportable surplus.

In Eastern and Middle Norway the average farmer owns about thirty acres on which he raises some twenty cows, two horses, supports a family of several children and provides a living for his farm hands — an accomplishment made possible by intensive methods of cultivation and a high degree of mechanization.

Well-kept white farmhouses and outbuildings in red, located in the midst of the fields, give an air of peaceful prosperity. Located at a sufficient distance from his neighbours, the Norwegian farmer has his own little kingdom — made beautiful by carefully tended flower beds and kitchen gardens.

Forests fringe the farm, bringing extra revenue for little luxuries for the wife and children. Seeding is done in May and the crops are harvested in August and September. Long Summer days provide a rapid growing season which accounts in large measure for the bountiful crops. Big, spacious barns protect the harvest until the threshing in November. In the Western and Northern parts of Norway nature is not so kind. The average farm is smaller, about five or six acres, and very rocky. Fishing usually supplements the family income. It is said that, if a man from the East settles down in the West, he will live as long as the food he brought with him will last. On the other

'Skjenk''—a cabinet in country farmhouse, hand-painted in gay colors. Hand-made wooden spoons and pewter utensils are typical.

The eldest son, who ordinarily takes over the farm, often goes through High School and School of Agriculture, even the University of Agriculture, providing him with advanced knowledge of animal husbandry and the science of efficient cultivation and forestry. The other children may "marry farms" or buy new ones, or go to town where a host of occupations beckon.

Farmers have a surprising knowledge of, and interest in, the laws of the land. This knowledge may stand them in good stead if their lawyer should prove inadequate in winning the case.

Even the smallest farmer with a handful of acres, no forest, a limited education and only one horse invariably will have the latest type of American- or Canadian-made plow. As you watch him behind the plow on a beautiful Spring day, as he pauses in the fresh furrows for the cool drink brought to him by his devoted wife, accompanied by a youngster hanging to her skirt, you know that he is supremely happy — contented — with no wish but to live, work and die on that very spot. That is the personification of peaceful, substantial Norway.

Farm in Eastern Norway. The rolling land and big red barns are in contrast to those found in Western Norway.

Occasionally the son does not live up to his father's expectations. Get-rich-quick investments, squandering of hard-earned money in town and other pursuits beyond the realm of farming may result in bankruptcy and the loss of his farm. However, the law protects the "Marrow of the Nation" by making it possible to redeem the farm which has been sold for bankruptcy within five years, so that it will not pass out of the hands of the family provided that it has been within the hands of the family for more than twenty years. This measure of legal protection gives a picture of the traditions of Nordic farm civilization.

The pulley used to carry milk and produce ou[t] valley illustrates the more difficult farming co[nditions] found in Western Norway.

Pre-war farming in Norway.

University of Agriculture near *Oslo* is responsible for the improved standards in farming.

FISHERIES ARE WORLD FAMOUS

Ola didn't have to describe the familiar tin of Norwegian sardines, which, in normal times, may be found in practically every grocery store. Other phases of Norwegian fisheries were not so well known.

Before the war, dried, salted and frozen Norwegian fish were famous for their fine quality throughout the countries of Europe and far away in Africa and South America. The warm waters of the Gulf Stream and the thousands of miles of coast-line make the shores of Norway a favourite spawning and feeding ground for practically every fish known to the North Atlantic.

For the most part the smaller fishing craft are owned by the fishermen themselves and operated on a share basis. In the larger vessels the crew shares in the catch, encouraging maximum effort.

Fishing nets and floats frame this quaint harbour at *Lofoten*.

"Silver" from the sea — fish — one of Norway's great resources.

The Norwegian fishing fleet is modern, consisting of about 30,000 small motor-powered vessels. The yearly catch, about one million tons, was almost on a level with that of Great Britain before the war, and made Norway famous as the "home" of cod liver oil.

Careful handling, modern equipment, and the co-operation of the Norwegian Government through meteorological reports, supervision of fishermen's agreements, State Insurance, State Bonds for financing, State Fisheries studying fish habits and rigid standards of quality and size, all combine to ease the lot of the fishermen and to place Norwegian fish at a premium in the markets of the world.

The fishing fleet at *Lofoten*, showing the many types of vessels used.

SEALING AND WHALING

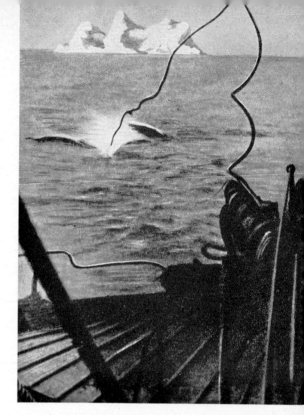

Left to right—An old Harp Seal, which has undoubtedly spent many seasons migrating thousands of miles back and forth between the open sea and the pack ice, where the young are born.

Sealing ships meeting at the edge of the ice for an exchange of news and plans.

Left to right—Hauling the seal up on to the ice floe.

A baby seal.

The waters around the South Pole and the North Pole are equally familiar to Norway's sealing and whaling fleet. The pictures on this page show many of the scenes common to the everday life of the Norwegian sailor aboard the whaling ship.

The whale brought aboard. The tremendous size is indicated by this picture.

Shooting the harpoon — *a direct hit!*

Bringing the whale aboard through the "slip" —a special device found only on whaling ships.

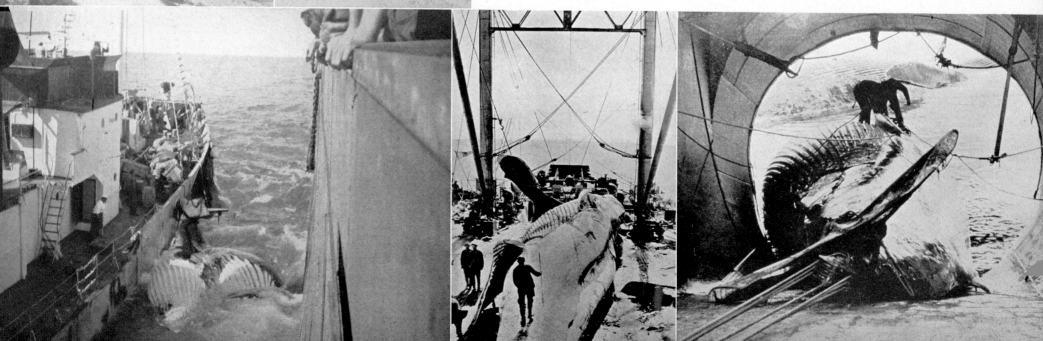

INDUSTRIAL NORWAY

This was one phase of Norwegian life Ola always found interesting to his Canadian and American hosts.

Along the fjord-studded West Coast the visitor to Norway would scarcely think of Norway as a modern industrialized country. This is due to the fact that one-fifth of Norwegian industry is concentrated mostly in the South-eastern part of the country. Even in the industrial centres there is not the usual smoky evidence of industrial activity, due to the fact that Norwegian industry is highly electrified.

Anti-trust laws prevent the concentration of big business in the hands of a few persons. Limited stock companies are popular because they tend to distribute the profits to more hands. The co-operative spread rapidly before the war. The banking system, following diffculties similar to other countries, was more centralized.

The most important Norwegian industries are related to the processing of natural resources, such as lumber, pulp and paper, stone, fish-canning and fishing equipment. Mining and the metallurgical industries requiring great quantities of electricity also contribute to Norway's wealth, assuring a solid foundation for expansion in the postwar period.

Shipbuilding, naturally, was an important industry due to the demands of the Norwegian Merchant Marine for modern vessels, sixty per cent of which were motor ships before the war. These very latest types built in Norway were in large measure helpful in raising Norwegian shipping to its prominent place in world trade.

Developments during the war in the science of light metals promise a bright future for Norway's aluminum industry, with the abundant supplies of electric power which are available.

Automobiles and equipment requiring mass production based on a mass market never have gained a place in Norwegian industry. Limited population and the efficiency of Canadian and American manufacturers will mean a continued excellent market for these products after the war in exchange for Norway's products of the sea, forest, land or mine.

The art of shipbuilding is as old as Norway.

Aluminum and chemical plants thrive where power is plentiful.

Norwegian paper mill (top). *Sarpsborg* Bridge in East Norway. *Skjeggefoss* (lower left). Thousands of waterfalls—"White Coal"—supply abundant electric power for her growing industries. Two electric power plants (centre below). Going up in one of Norway's famous cable cars (lower right).

spring thaw the exciting game begins for the loggers starting the timber down the rivers, streams and waterfalls. Norwegian forests are privately owned, mainly by the farmers. Thus they get a good income in cash, in additon to what they earn from the farm.

The Norwegian lumberjacks and loggers are a popular type among the people. The hard and often exciting life these men have lived for generations in the forests have been immortalized in Norwegian literature. In the latter years the lumberjacks have been famous in sport, winning the highest prizes in national and international ski competitions.

Marking trees for cutting. Modern forestry methods are practiced to preserve the fine forests.

Soup's on! Enjoying a well earned rest in the woods.

LUMBER INDUSTRY

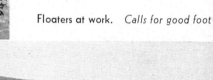

Floaters at work. *Calls for good foot*

"BEYOND SING THE WOODS"

Norwegian forests cover about 35% of the country. The total export of pulp, paper and cellulose amounts to more than one million tons, representing about 15% of the total world production and more than a hundred million dollars a year in income for the nation. Reforestation is carried on extensively and regulated by law. No one is allowed to cut more timber each year than the estimated new crop of saplings, thus preventing any scarcity in the future. The lumber industry gives work to thousands of people cutting and taking the logs down to the numerous rivers which take the timber hundreds of miles through the valleys down to the lakes and the coast to the the pulp and paper mills. Seventy per cent of the Norwegian forests consist of pine and spruce trees. In the autumn and winter months the trees are cut and transported by tractor or horses to the frozen rivers and with the

Hauling logs to river bank, ready for the Spring.

Seagulls basking in the Midnight Sun.

OTHER ATTRACTIONS FOR THE VISITOR

In a land such as this with rapid glacier-fed streams, thousands of acres of forest, ski slopes unparalleled anywhere in the world, splendid modern roads carved out of the mountains and a coast washed all year 'round by warm water, there is the making of every conceivable sport and recreation. Little wonder that Norway was attracting every year an increasing number to thrill to her variety of attractions, providing a total yearly revenue in excess of twenty million dollars. People came from almost every part of the world, some more typical in their vacation hobbies than others. If a Norwegian leaving on his own vacation saw a man standing in a river fishing salmon, and he, on his return three weeks later discovered the same man standing in the same spot fishing salmon, then he would know that the Englishman had arrived.

Air travel, and future developments in transportation, will bring this "Land of the Midnight Sun" within easy reach of all.

NORWAY — THE TOURISTS' PARADISE

Practically the whole of Norway, if placed in the Western Hemisphere, would resemble a great National Park.

In Southern Norway, in Summer, swimming is enjoyed along the beaches, while, not half an hour away by plane, unsurpassed skiing may be had. Modern tourist hotels in the mountains and along the coast cater to every need of the tourist. Trains, streamlined buses and coastal steamers will take you to your destination quickly and comfortably.

The tourist business has grown with the development and expansion of communications. This has been an extremely expensive undertaking, similar to that of building roads and railways through the Rocky Mountains. It has been financed by the government. The main populated centres are fairly well connected by railroads and highways, some of the marvellous feats of engineering. As most of the towns are along the coast, the heavy traffic goes by ship. Shipping companies are privately owned. In the extreme north, steamers are the only means of communication, except for an airline. Plans for railroads and highways were under way before the invasion.

The country was also connected with the outside world by airline to Sweden, Holland and Scotland. Due to the expense involved in flattening the rocky country for airdromes, the inter-Norway line was equipped with seaplanes which followed the coastline. The only company for air traffic was subsidized by the government. A limited number of private companies for taxi and sports flying also existed.

LAND OF THE MIDNIGHT SUN

No one ever thinks of Norway without associating it with the midnight sun. For example, at Tromsö from May 23rd to July 20th, and, further North, at the North Cape from May 12th to July 29th, the sun never sets. Thus, for twenty-four hours of the day, from the deck of a Norwegian or British tourist liner, the visitor can enjoy the indescribably beautiful fjords and the magic spell of this vast, peaceful country of forest, land and water.

A lofty *seter* (mountain farm).

Seterjente— Farm girl

Kylling Bridge near *Romsdal* illustrates the engineering feats necessary to build Norwegian railroads.

RAIL AND ROADS WERE EXPENSIVE TO BUILD

Meditation in *Nordmarka* — Norway's great natural park north of *Oslo* on a plateau rising from the fjord.

Down . . . down . . . down . . . straight down. Thrilling sights like this are common.

The contrast of nature from rugged mountains to the silence of lake and forest inspire the magic tales.

The fisherman's paradise.

NORSE MYTHOLOGY

Sometimes for diversion Ola would tell the tales of Norway—the romantic stories dear to every Norwegian—of *Thor, Balder* and *Loke*—gods of the past.

The more imaginative are invariably lured by these magic tales of Norse Mythology . . . the mysteries of the great forests . . . the stories of the elves . . . funny, "human animals" and the dwarfs dwelling below the ground. Charming are the tales of the King of the Forest, Mr. Bear . . . the Gangster, Mr. Wolf . . . the Lawyer, Mr. Fox . . . and the Lonesome Rabbit who only managed to scare the frogs . . . and, of course, hidden by soft leaves and the yellow water flowers of the lakes, sits *Nökken* the old ghost with burning eyes and face like an old twisted root peering out at these creatures of the forest.

In the mountains we find the ogres and trolls that have become the folk-lore of the natives—a source of the stories which never fail to charm the visitor. So much have they become part of the people, particularly in the less accessible parts of the country, that you almost feel that the stories and strange characters are real.

Then there's *Huldra* the wood-nymph. Be careful she doesn't lure you into the ogre mountains, from which you will never escape unless you shout the magic holy words which return you to reality. You may discover, however, that she will be one of those lovely girls living in cottages in the mountains. She is watching over the herds of cows grazing in the highland during the summer. In fact, you may find her very sweet, very blond, with very, very blue eyes—known all over the world, often pictured on the tourist posters as "*seterjente*", with her little cottage and two goats—ready to serve you with coffee and cream "so thick it can almost stand by itself."

"Born on skiis."

A nation of ski competitors. Start of the famous *Birkebeinerrenn*

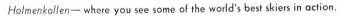

Holmenkollen— where you see some of the world's best skiers in action.

SKIING AND OTHER SPORTS

On skis Ola was the marvel of all Canadians. He explained why.

Although Norwegians were familiar with skiing before the year 1200, it did not become universally popular with men until the late part of the Nineteenth Century—due to a great extent to *Fridtjof Nansen's* skiing exploits.

Girls, not to be out-done, followed suit and gained proficiency in the art and were able to take their place with the men on the enjoyable ski week-ends which were such a popular part of Norwegian life.

And the older generation! Every man under eighty still thinks of himself as a "hunter," and, therefore, finds this people's sport almost a necessity.

At the Olympic Games the Norwegian skiers have brought home the highest honors in almost every competition.

More than 100,000 people from all parts of the country, headed by the Royal Family, gathered every year for the classic competitions at *Holmenkollen*, famous ski jump outside *Oslo.*

Speed and figure skating are other favourite Winter sports. In the Summer soccer is the most popular game, followed by track sports, swimming and marathon running through the forest with compass. Boxing and wrestling are popular spectator sports. Fresh air, exercise, sunshine and life in the open are almost a religion and are responsible in large part for the good health enjoyed by the people.

NORWEGIAN FOOD

Canadians and Americans were anxious to hear of Norway's famous dishes and pastries. Ola always had an eager audience. Yes, coffee is the national drink and the thick Norwegian cream almost a tradition. The daily menu is similar in many ways to the Canadian and American, with perhaps greater emphasis on gravies and milk.

Famous national dishes, such as entrées like *Labskaus, Lutefisk, Får-i-kål, Kjöttkake, Fiskekake*, and pastries including *Blötkake, Sandkake* and *Smultringer*, never fail to tempt the visitor, and, when mentioned to a Norwegian, always make his mouth water.

NORDIC CUSTOMS

Dancing was similar to that in North America, with the exception that "hot" Harlem rhythm usually was a little out of keeping with the Norwegian temperament. Folk dancing, especially on Independence Day, May 17th, was enjoyed throughout the land.

Independence Day is always a marvellous sight with the parades of all ages, thousands of flags, school children's bands with tiny, red-faced trumpeters passing in a seemingly endless procession before the Royal Castle.

There were no great class distinctions in Norway. Everyone thinks he is equal to the other, regardless of money, and only willing to recognize the superiority of those who show an outstanding interest in

Pre-war, carefree pleasure in the Oslofjord.

Norwegian sailors in keen competition — the annual *Hankö* Regatta.

Crown Prince Olav — "The Sailor Prince."

the promotion of projects beneficial to the nation as a whole. This was particularly well exemplified in the motto of King Haakon, *"Alt for Norge"* (All for Norway).

Christmas Eve is for the children! It begins with a march around the Christmas Tree, singing the old, familiar Christmas Carols, followed by the distribution of gifts from *Julenissen* — the Norwegian Santa Claus. One of the old customs prevailing in the country was to place a huge bowl of porridge in the hayloft for his refreshment in return for the gifts he brought.

Not to be forgotten, of course, are the sheaves of grain placed on the roofs to supply food to the brown sparrows which are so dear to the hearts of all Norwegians.

Easter brings an exodus from the cities to the high mountains, where the city folk acquire the first sunburn of the season, skiing.

Political and social clubs play a part in the life of the Norwegian, indicating a live interest in the affairs of the day. Students' associations at the universities play an important part in this respect.

Horse-racing may be mentioned chiefly as a hobby of ship-owners, especially those of English descent who can say "boat" with such an Oxford accent that you can see twenty generations of the House of Lords beneath the Norwegian exterior.

In sailing races, naturally, the Norwegians show a real prowess, winning fame throughout the world. The little island of *Hankö* in *Oslofjord*, before the war, was the centre of international sailing races every year—the virtual gathering place of the world's most famous and enthusiastic sailors.

Restaurants close by one o'clock in the morning. There are no night clubs. However, entertainment continues in private homes for those too much alive for bed.

Liquor sales are monopolized by the government and follow district regulations. Some districts are dry. In others, such as *Oslo*, liquor can be purchased up to five o'clock on weekdays and one o'clock on Saturdays. Restaurants serve liquor. Scotch whisky is in greatest demand, although quantities of wine were imported from France, Spain and Italy before the war in exchange for fish. *Aquavita*, the national fire-water distilled from potatoes and grain, is a quick way to the Kingdom of Bacchus. Beer also is available as a national contribution to "the floating empire".

Bergen with the old section of the city in the background.

Trondheim, world famous for its ancient cathedral and technical university.

NORWEGIAN CITIES

"Visit our cities. You'll be surprised how modern some of them are," said Ola in speaking of urban Norwegian life.

The most ancient Norwegian town is *Tönsberg*, which is more than 1,000 years old.

Oslo, the capital, *Trondheim* and *Bergen* date from the early Middle Ages, and, along with many others, naturally have quite a tradition.

Oslo, is the largest, with a total population of about 300,000 while the others range from 100,000 down. Most of these are surrounded by fjords, hills and mountains, with forests creeping right down into the towns.

Modern Norwegian architecture is changing the face of the cities, "Walls of Windows" are a noteworthy feature of this new trend. Skyscrapers, such as those of North America, are unknown. The importance of parks and flower gardens is stressed in all modern city planning. "Back yards" are disappearing rapidly, leaving room for more inviting and more comfortable living arrangements.

Cleanliness is characteristic. Large water carts flush the streets daily, sometimes several times a day in Summer, followed by special sweeping cars that remove the balance of the dirt. Buildings are scrubbed even on the outside to keep the "face of the town" clean and orderly.

In normal times, one glance down the streets of the city shows the usual street-cars, busses, taxis and private cars. *Oslo* boasts a three-minute subway, which, before the war, was planned to be extended. This subway joins the heart of the city to the chief suburban terminal—the gateway to *Nordmarka*, the sports paradise. Long lines of young people from three years to eighty crowd the station for the week-end, which lasts usually from Saturday noon to Monday morning.

Comfortable electric trains whisk you up 1,500 feet in thirty minutes and leave you deep in the forest for hiking in Summer and skiing in Winter.

Through the suburbs you pass by residences of the most modern architecture found anywhere, veritable glass houses, with electric heating concealed in the walls. In spite of the efficiency and convenience of this method of heating, the fireplace remains an unchangeable part of the Norwegian home. Roses, apple trees, pear trees and prune trees, and beds of flowers make these homes of the Norwegian business man a place of happy relaxation.

The business section of *Oslo* showing the modern office buildings with the National Theatre on the left.

The Harbour.

Business section.

CITY OF BERGEN

Ancient castle.

Funicular train to the mountains.

Old and new architecture at one of *Oslo's* market places.

Akershus — ancient fortress and castle in *Oslofjord*.

OSLO, CAPITAL CITY OF NORWAY

The new City Hall — in the latest Norwegian modern architecture.

Deichman Library centrally located in *Oslo*

The "Oslo Princess" chosen on Oslo Day.

She skiis with the best of them.

The home of skiing. Norwegian girls take their place beside the men on the ski trails enjoying to the full this thrilling, healthful sport which Norwegians have made famous throughout the world.

MISS NORWAY

Ola thought to flatter Canadian and American girls by comparing them with his Norwegian sisters.

Miss or Mrs. Norway enjoys the rights of men, with the exceptions that she cannot serve in the army or become a minister. It has been suggested that the reason for the military restriction may be to prevent the soldiers fighting among themselves instead of with the enemy, while the clerical restrictions may be based on the words of St. Paul, who believed that women should not speak in public gatherings.

As a matter of fact, Miss Norway prefers to rule by her feminine charm. She feels most fatally fascinating in the latest evening dress from Paris, which city before the war was considered supreme in matters of fashion. However, Miss Norway prefers to temper the French mental "it" in keeping with her calmer Nordic nature—no doubt, too, in order to keep in step with her fellow-countrymen who find themselves irresistible in the latest English fashions for men.

Miss Norway is as independent as any American or Canadian girl, not bound to traditional customs which she considers unreasonable. She will be very informal and friendly the first time she meets you but cools off quickly if you should think it means more than "how do you do." For the most part her nature is romantic and unbusiness-like, very much like that of her Canadian sisters. She likes to be accepted as a comrade who can take care of herself. She might be symbolized as a girl with a piece of earth in one hand and a lipstick in the other; as a healthy combination of nature and civilization.

She prefers to be married, as most women do, but it is far from a necessity as almost all girls have an occupation—from maids to doctors, lawyers and professors. It is a "plus" for a Norwegian girl that she works, indicating that she will be able to understand not only a man's love, but also his problems. The statement, "I don't *need* to work", on the lips of a Norwegian maiden is "out of bounds" and has no place in modern Norwegian life.

A married woman has a strong position in the home. Divorce is fairly easy to get if both agree. If they don't, or if there are children, it is more complicated. The number of divorces is not very high compared to many other nations. Family life is considered the main foundation of the nation.

HEALTH

You only had to look at Ola to realize the place that health plays in the education of the Norwegian youth.

In rural districts the midwife usually assists the stork, but, when the mother is within reach of town, modern maternity hospitals are used. The latest discoveries in nutrition and the newest methods of child training were practised by the majority. Health of the child is uppermost in the mother's mind, giving rise to a statement to a doctor such as this, "I have followed the instructions in the book so carefully that the only reason for the child being unwell must be that there is a mistake in the printing."

Norway is well provided with hospitals organized and financed by the local or national government. These hospitals are the pride of the nation and rank among the most modern in the world. Tuberculosis and cancer, the worst enemies of the nation, have been fought with great success.

General health is good, with the average span of life high. Those who live to be a hundred usually brag at never having seen a doctor in their lives.

EDUCATION

"Yes, I had to go to school 7 years. English was a part of my education," said Ola in telling of his education.

According to Norwegian law, every child who reaches the age of seven must attend school for 7 years. In the last two years all children are taught English. Girls are taught cooking and the science of nutrition along the lines of the latest discoveries in vitamins. Schooling, including all text-books and materials, is free.

In several parts of the country, especially in *Oslo*, children are given breakfast at school. The so-called "*Oslo* breakfast" consisting of milk, whole wheat bread, dark bread, butter, cheese, porridge and raw fruit and vegetables is ideal according to moden theories of nutrition.

About fifty per cent of the children in Public School proceed to High School for three years, and about fifty per cent of these go on to College for an additional three years where they continue along three types of courses, all of which include English, French, German and mathematics. The Classic course also includes Latin and Greek—Mathematics, which is the foundation for scientific study also includes physics and chemistry—and Commercial, including business education and Spanish. After College the student goes to one of several Universities to study law, medicine, engineering, agriculture or whatever profession he has chosen. Special evening schools are organized throughout the country.

Education in the high schools, and even in the universities, is free, although the text-books are not. Training for the customary professions takes place at the universities, while special schools provide advanced education in business, technical and agricultural studies.

The government underwrites all the operational expenses of the universities. The school buildings dominate the town, standing as monuments to the nation's respect for learning. You will find many Norwegian names among leading experts in the European and American scientific world.

LITERATURE

Ludvig Holberg's highly satirical comedies of the early Eighteenth Century form the connecting link between old Norse and modern Norwegian literature.

The "big four" of the Nineteenth Century Norwegian literature . . . *Henrik Ibsen, Björnstierne Björnson, Alexander Kielland and Jonas Lie* . . . represent the apex of this golden age. *Björnson* was awarded the literary Nobel prize.

These men influenced the life of the nation. The satirical, internationally-minded *Ibsen* created the immortal "*Peer Gynt*", showing the author's peculiarly Norwegian reactions to situations in Norway and the world as well. *Ibsen* amuses his readers,

Even the smaller towns have large modern hospitals to serve the surrounding districts. This hospital is at *Bodö* which was levelled to the ground by the Germans.

and himself, by showing up the customary ways in which we try to escape our bad conscience.

Björnson discovered the Norwegian farmer and glorified him with the distinction "the Marrow of the Nation". He wrote the libretto for the National Anthem, "Yes We Love This Land of Ours", set to music by *Richard Nordraak*, famous Norwegian composer.

Jonas Lie wrote of the family, depicting the head of the house in all his glory and limited superiority compared with his wife, who, often in reality, rules the roost.

Kielland represented the elegant writer, holding his pen in the latest fashionable Parisian gloves and getting a great kick out of small-minded people's great quarrels over nothing. He enjoyed putting the old-fashioned school system on the sharp tip of his pen. *Kielland's* flirting style and his innuendo between the lines have won a place for him in all Norwegian hearts, symbolizing the entertaining writer who struggled for cultural progress within the nation. His heart belongs to the Norwegian sailors and his book, "Skipper Worse", is an immortal, smiling hymn to the modern peaceful Viking of the Seven Seas.

In addition to these internationally-famous writers of the Nineteenth Century there were numerous other writers and poets. The literary productivity may be due to the long dark Autumn and Winter nights which give plenty of opportunity for thought and self-expression. As aptly expressed by a fisherman when asked what he did through the long Winter nights, he said, "We just sit and think . . . sometimes we just sit".

MUSIC AND PAINTING

Music and painting kept pace with the golden age in literature. *Edvard Grieg* expressed in music what the writers depicted in words. He grasped the essential atmosphere of the nation's love of Norwegian nature and interest in ogres.

Ole Bull, gifted violinist and composer, contributed to the musical awakening of Norway in the Nineteenth Century. *Johan Svendsen's* world-famous rhapsodies and *Christian Sinding's* arrangements of Norwegian folk songs are particularly noteworthy. The greatest living Norwegian artist is *Edvard Munch*, who interprets a healthy, social-minded realism with an inspiring impressiveness. He has exerted a strong influence on Norwegian art.

Monumental murals, mostly in official buildings by such men as *Henrik Sorensen*, *Axel Revold* and *Per Krogh* are prominent features of modern Norwegian art. Among the sculptors are *Gustav Vigeland*, whose fountain project in *Oslo* was practically completed before the war.

Art institutions are on the look-out for talent and great effort is made to discover young artists and offer practical assistance in their development.

Before the war the press was modern and busy, and quite American in appearance. Numerous newspapers, political and non-political, reflected all phases of Norwegian life. A great interest in all things national and international was common.

Mural by *Axel Revold*

Outspoken and free, the press of Norway was a constant safeguard against corruption and an enemy of the very ideologies that were to try to engulf the world. To the press, then, can be credited in part the rapid progress of the country and the introduction of a host of benefits and social reforms.

THEATRE AND ENTERTAINMENT

Ola, in speaking of the theatre, would say, "The classical theatre always has enjoyed a great tradition, particularly in the large centres. Classic plays, modern comedies, the opera and operettas are popular. The comedies of *Holberg* and the plays of *Ibsen* and Shakespeare are perennial favourites. You've seen them here in America, I'm sure."

Theatres in the lighter vein, commenting on the events of the day through popular songs, jokes, satire, sentimental songs and chorus girls, are extremely popular.

Movies over-shadow all other forms of entertainment. Large streamlined halls in the cities and the small meeting houses in the country bring this popular entertainment to all.

American, English, French and German movies were most common before the war. As everyone learns English and German in the last two years at public school, most Norwegians understand these with the help of a few dialogue translations appearing on the screen. Norway was very close to Hollywood and America through the medium of the movie and radio, learning the latest songs almost as quickly as they were introduced.

The Norwegian radio and movies were financed and controlled by the government, which realized the important cultural place this medium holds in the life of the nation.

Painting by *Edvard Munch*

Gustav Vigeland in his Studio

Fridtjof Nansen on skiis.

EXPLORATION

In the field of exploration Ola didn't have to introduce these famous Norwegians. *Roald Amundsen*, famous Norwegian explorer, first discovered the South Pole and later reached the North Pole by dirigible. He was typical of that famous breed of men who never give up and who year after year by sheer determination and persistence have rolled back the boundaries of the known world.

Fridtjof Nansen, with his little ship *"Fram"*, is another who has won an undying place in the hearts of the Norwegian people — symbolizing as he does many of the attractive characteristics of Norwegians.

A towering giant of a man, face like an untouched mountain peak, wild blond hair and big blue eyes, Nansen never failed to remind you of the giant in the Norwegian saga. An outstanding scientist, he was internationally known for his relief work among suffering Armenians and Russians which will stand always as one of the brightest chapters in the history of mankind.

RELIGION

Ola was proud of his Christian background.

Ninety-six per cent of the Norwegian people are Lutheran Protestant. The church is administered by the government. The Bishops and Ministers, who must have a university degree, are appointed to their positions by the government.

Sports Churches have sprung up in the forests. Ministers ski to their Sunday morning service in Winter and hike, with their vestments in a knapsack, in Summer.

Freedom of religion is absolute. When the various church bodies faced the Nazi enemy they forgot their differences in a Christian determination to fight for the abiding truth and fundamental values of Christianity, common to them all.

THE STANDARD OF LIVING

"We live well. We're happy. We're not greedy for others' goods," Ola often repeated.

The standard of living in Norway prior to the war was one of the highest in the world. Extreme wealth and poverty did not exist. Slums were not to be found. Competition is free and usually keen. The principle of taxation is similar to that in England where extremely large incomes are taxed and the funds thus received turned back for the benefit of the nation as a whole. Taxes on luxuries are heavy. Necessities of life, on the other hand, are kept low in price to protect the interest of the farmer and the average man on the street.

Often the worker owns his own house and garden located outside the city. Furniture and decorations are in good taste. A car or motorboat, although not of the latest model, is often enjoyed by the worker.

Before the war vacations were common for all. They were spent along the coast or up in the mountains; the family usually migrating to some resort for the Summer while father had to commute back and forth for week-ends.

Relief for the unemployed was granted as early as 1900. Insurance for all workers entitled them to free medical treatment, free hospitalization and benefits up to sixty per cent of their wages during absence because of sickness.

Unemployment funds subsidized by the government with compulsory membership provided a pension at the age of seventy. All industrial workers received two weeks' vacation with full pay. Accident insurance and pensions for the blind and crippled were provided. Compulsory insurance was in effect for all workers earning less than $3,000 a year in the form of a payroll deduction. Medical and dental care were provided.

Much welfare was also organized privately.

Trade unions working in increasing understanding with manufacturers' associations achieved mutual agreements and made possible many of the benefits mentioned.

Live and let live — serve and not rule, was the Norwegian greeting to the world. Norway's high social standard as a modern democracy was won by generations of peaceful effort. For the future they nourished one desire: Peace. They believed that no problem was so great that it had to be solved by war. They had no enemies and no demands.

To the Norwegian also, his home is his castle.

MODERN HOMES IN NORWAY

present some of the latest developments in architecture, altogether giving an impression of a hymn to the sunshine—the eternal fire—and the latest discoveries in modern comfort.

City Apartments

Suburban Home

Living-Rooms in city homes

WAR

No age limit for soldiers.

In speaking of the war and his own personal experiences, Ola always said, "April 9th, 1940, will live long in the memory of Norwegians."

Suddenly, cruelly, without warning or provocation, the Germans broke the peace — a peace which had lasted more than 125 years. By sea and by air they came in hordes bent on the quick, immediate collapse and subjection of the country. Thousands of them, who, as children some twenty years before, had been invited to the country to recover from starvation after the first Great War, now returned to kill, capture and enslave those who had treated them as their own children.

Planes, hundreds of them, bearing their black, ugly Swastikas appeared dropping bombs indiscriminately in an attempt to shatter and demoralize resistance.

The small Norwegian Navy and coastal fortresses sank several German warships. A handful of dauntless Norwegian pilots, hopelessly outnumbered, shot down many enemy planes. Mobilization was difficult. The government set up new headquarters and defence lines were established. Thousands escaped to join the Norwegian Forces. Officers rose to the occasion commanding units they had never seen before. A tunic, a gun and a few instructions and these boys were off to fight and die. Heroes were made every minute.

They stopped the German army unaided for three weeks. The Allies arrived, but complete superiority in tanks, artillery and planes forced a withdrawal to Northern Norway. Here the fighting lasted another month before active resistance on Norwegian soil had to end.

It cost the Germans more than 60,000 men and one-third of their fleet, plus a precious two months' time. Later events have indicated that perhaps these losses were even more decisive than believed at that time.

They held.

The Nazi came. Destruction followed.

Bomb shelter.

Throughout the sixty-two days the Royal Norwegian Army and Naval Air Forces fought bitterly. Fighters, reconnaissance and light bomber squadrons gave a good account of themselves against staggering odds.

Joined by the R.A.F. after the first three weeks, the Norwegian Air Force fought on and when the end came retired to England at the request of the R.A.F. commanding officer and the Norwegian Government.

General *Otto Ruge*, Commander-in-Chief, now prisoner of war. His name will live in the memory of all Norwegians.

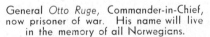

Every man does his duty voluntarily.

WAR

The Norwegian government-in-exile already had plans under way for the re-organization of the Air Force. Plans for a training centre in France were abandoned with the fall of France. Instead, negotiations were begun with Canadian authorities, resulting in the establishment of "Little Norway" in Toronto.

The fight in Norway ended in June, 1940. By August, the Canadian site was chosen and by November the camp opened. Among the thousands of Norwegian youths who escaped to join the Norwegian Army and Navy in England, hundreds continued to Camp "Little Norway." Most of these escaped either by way of the North Sea or through Sweden and around the world through Russia and India.

The first Norwegian unit went overseas in April, 1941, to Iceland. The first all-Norwegian fighter squadron with complete air and ground crew arrived in England in June 1941.

To-day, the Royal Norwegian Air Force consists of patrol bomber units based on Iceland; fighter squadrons and a Catalina unit located in England. Individual members serve with the R.A.F. Fighter, Night Fighter and Bomber units and in the Ferry Command.

In action, Norwegian pilots have proved the equal of any other. One squadron at Dieppe had the highest score of any Allied squadron in that historic battle, shooting down nine enemy planes and damaging seven without the loss of a single plane. Two Norwegian squadrons accounted for a total of sixteen planes and eleven damaged with a loss of four.

Following an engagement over France in which one Norwegian squadron accounted for seven of ten planes destroyed, the English Wing Commander for the Norwegian squadrons in action made the statement that "There are no better fighting squadrons in Southern England to-day". Other statements are quoted as follows: for instance, from Associated Press, "Among the most daring and skilful Allied pilots are the Norwegians. After escaping from home, most of them went from England to Canada for training at 'Little Norway', their huge flying school at Toronto. Now they form a powerful unit in the R.A.F., operating from bases in Iceland, as well as Britain.

"Iceland, with its tricky winds of frequent gale velocity, fast-descending fogs, quickly changeable weather and barren, mountainous terrain, presents some of the world's worst flying conditions."

Norwegian bombers based on Iceland continued the fight.

Squadrons of the Royal Norwegian Air Force had another big day on Friday, March 12, 1943, when they were sent aloft to battle 24 German planes which were attempting a daylight raid on London. Without suffering any losses themselves, the Norwegians succeeded in shooting down six of the raiders, and in addition scoring two "probables" and five "damaged". The following day London newspapers stated that all of the raiders shot down were bagged by Norwegian planes, and the London "Daily Sketch" added: "With the exception of a few contemptible Quislings, this will arouse intense satisfaction in all Norwegians, as indeed it does in all Britons. That Norwegians should be fighting, and fighting so bravely on our side to-day brings the historical wheel to a full circle. When Vikings hundreds of years ago pushed their prows into their icy seas in quest of adventure and new lands, many of them ended their journey via France in Britain. Therefore, there is a strong strain of Norwegian blood in our veins to-day, and after a thousand years the two strains, the old and the new, meet and mingle to the undoing of the common foe."

On the 17th of May, 1943, the British Minister for Air, Sir Archibald Sinclair, declared that since March 3rd, one Norwegian fighter squadron had the highest score of all the squadrons in the R.A.F.

By July 1943, the R.N.A.F. fighter squadrons alone had shot down, destroyed and damaged many more German planes than the Royal Norwegian Air Force had at the outset of the war—counted in three figures. The R.N.A.F. bomber crews have dropped more bombs on German and enemy objectives than the Germans dropped on Norway during the whole of the 62 days of active resistance.

More than a year ago the main Training Centre, "Little Norway", was increased by the establishment of a second Training Centre for elementary flying at Muskoka

Guarding the Northern sea lane.

Airport, 120 miles from Toronto, with a Recruiting and Recreation centre 60 miles farther North (180 miles from Toronto) called "Vesle Skaugum".

After the conclusion of a favourable financial agreement with the Royal Canadian Air Force, the main centre, "Little Norway", has been transferred to Muskoka Airport, which was enlarged to meet the need for more living quarters and training activities. The "Little Norway" camp has been bought by the Canadian military authorities, but the aerodrome connected with the Camp will still be at the disposal of the Norwegians. The training of new air and ground crew to supply and increase the fighting units overseas is proceeding at the new centre and under even better conditions than before. All the activities in the Air Force, including training equipment and planes, are paid for by the Norwegian government-in-exile in London. They get the money from the income of the Norwegian Merchant Marine.

According to a British statement, this Merchant Marine has supplied Great Britain with fifty per cent of her oil and one-third of her foodstuffs during the war. The Norwegian government also is paying for all Norwegian military activities overseas, including the Norwegian Army and Navy in action, amounting altogether to the sum of about $100,000,000 in American money — a year.

After the United States entered the war, the Norwegians, to a certain extent, received a lend-lease agreement on the background quoted from lend-lease agreement between Norwegians and Americans as follows: — "As the Norwegian Merchant Marine is of vital importance to the defense of the United States, the United States would put some of her immense resources at the disposal of the Norwegian government."

With their country occupied by enemies who have robbed it of all wealth, the Norwegian people within and outside the border have continued to fight against their oppressors with all means at their disposal. With that background, the Norwegians appreciate very much the proof of sympathy shown through the voluntary organizations assisting the Norwegian struggle to-day.

The Norwegian Air Force Training Centre in Canada alone has received about $400,000 in gifts for planes and military equipment and other activities in the training

WAR

The Norwegian Navy continued the fight from new bases in different parts of the world.

program. They have received a large part from Camp Little Norway Associations operating under license of the President's War Relief Control Board.

Among others who have taken interest in the Air Force, in addition to or apart from the Norwegian-Americans, the Swedish-Americans and the Danish-Americans must be mentioned. Yes, even the Finnish-Americans have sent contributions in expression of their admiration and sympathy. Large donations have been received from Norwegians in South America and from individuals of Norwegian descent in Guatemala, Mexico, Canada and the United States, and — last but not least — from the Americans and Canadians.

As a visible token of appreciation, the Air Force from time to time has asked the Royal Family — represented by Crown Prince *Olav*, Crown Princess *Märtha* and the Royal Children — to christen the gift planes of the Fairchild type bearing the names of the donors. Up to date, twenty-four planes have been christened. This squadron of gift planes will be transferred to Norway after the war as an historical proof of goodwill among people who try to help each other when the situation gives one party an opportunity to show that friendship can be a reality if you are really in need of it.

However, the greatest inspiration for every Norwegian fighting outside the borders to-day is the almost unbelievable resistance from the people at home. The Nazi hordes of eighty million over-ran this small nation of less than three million people by surprise and treachery. But up to the present they have not been able to conquer the nation. The hard and cruel life in this occupied country has shown, after weeks, months and years, that every patriotic Norwegian is a human fortress which cannot be conquered unless it is annihilated.

Not only the Norwegian Navy but also the Norwegian Merchant Marine has sunk Nazi U-boats on the high seas.

WAR

The fighters and bombers continue to attack German targets and shoot down enemy planes, operating from new bases in Britain. Their scores of Nazi planes can now be counted in three figures.

A Norwegian pilot receiving the O.B.E. (Order of British Empire), Civil Division

The ground crews have maintained the service, which has been considered by the R.A.F. as outstanding.

NORWEGIANS IN ICELAND TODAY

A thousand years ago many Norwegians settled in Iceland. Today their descendants, the Icelanders, welcome their Norwegian brothers to their churches and homes as a token of mutual sympathy.

Norwegian children who escaped with their parents from Norway have found a second home in Iceland.

Flying conditions over Iceland are considered among the worst in the world.

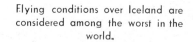

THE HOME FRONT

The German soldiers can suppress armed resistance but not the spirit indicated by "Live the King" imprinted in the snow.

Nazi guards ship loaded with Norwegian food seized for Germany.

And on the home front the resistance continues with unabated spirit—the great inspiration to those fighting outside the country.

If the Nazis close a church, the people hold services outside.

Life goes on in bombed cities in improvised buildings.

Bishop Berggrav and the famous author *Ronald Fangen* above in a serious discussion. Both are interned for their resistance.

After the last Russian offensive, which was followed with breathless interest in Norway, some Russian prisoners who were brought to Norway were transported from Oslo to *Lillehammer*. Two prisoners managed to escape during the trip and the Germans were hunting them. Passing a farmer, a German shouted, "Have you seen anything of the Russians?" "Russians in Norway," asked the farmer, "Good Lord, I didn't know they were advancing so quickly!"

One of the many examples of the unyielding will to resist on the home front is the story of a promising young athlete, who, after three weeks of unbelievable tortures, finally managed to throw himself from a window in order to shorten the time the Gestapo would take to kill him because he refused to speak or give information. A young pilot expressed his reaction as follows: "Everyone of us outside the country who is fighting with weapons needs only to think a second about him, and all the others at home who have suffered voluntarily in the same way. You will understand that we get a feeling which not only makes us anxious to fight, but makes it necessary for us to fight, to escape from a kind of internal explosion." This feeling also is explained in a British Wing Commander's words — "These Norwegian fighters are praying for the job every time there is a chance to go up and fight the enemy."

Norwegians of all ages are imprisoned in concentration camps. This shows *Grini* outside *Oslo* — one of the largest.

Med nordmenn for NORGE

GEFÄNGNIS GRINI.

Before we introduce you to the "Eagles' Nest" in pictures, we would in conclusion like to quote from a radio address given by a Norwegian pilot to the free Allied people: "We are not telling these stories about our people to boast. Of course, we are far from better than any other nation. But we are very anxious to tell the world that the Norwegian people to-day are making unlimited sacrifices to regain their freedom. They are glad to do so — voluntarily — because they have discovered that life doesn't mean anything without freedom. If our fate proves that you cannot sacrifice too much to prevent the loss of your freedom, our struggle will not have been in vain."

This is the story of Norway — the Norway that we have come to know, whose democratic spirit, independent traditions, love of freedom and undying courage have found a warm spot in our hearts, and which — thanks to Ola — will live long in our memory.

Warnings of their impending disaster face the Nazi invaders everywhere. The Norwegian people know that those fighting for justice and liberty will win. They don't hesitate to use every opportunity to taunt the enemy. This is clearly demonstrated by the imprint on the highway — "We will win."

"LITTLE NORWAY"
MUSKOKA

The goal of the long trip is the new "Little Norway," main training centre in Canada. Recruits continue to arrive, escaping from Norway to train for combat duty. They will reinforce the squadrons overseas.

"Norwegian Indians."

An ideal camp in homelike surroundings gives the recruits every opportunity to get into first-class condition.

The mascot of the camp enjoys riding in a jeep.

Summer and winter as in Norway.

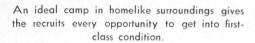

"Little Norway"
in pictures

R. N. A. F.
in Canada

H.M. KING HAAKON VII.

PILOT'S BADGE

OBSERVER'S BADGE

RADIO OPERATOR AND
AIR GUNNER'S BADGE

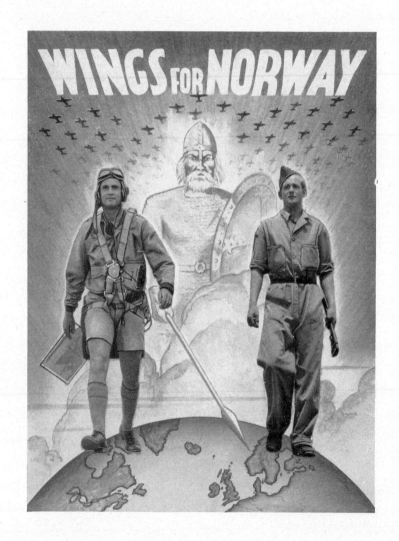

ESCAPING FROM NORWAY

in thousands, "the hard way" across the North Sea in fishing vessels after the two months' fight against overwhelming odds. They joined those who came the "easy way" around the world and reorganized their armed forces along with their King and Government-in-exile to continue the fight at sea, on land and in the air.

These are actual pictures taken by three boys who, after a 13-day fight with terrible storms on the North Sea, were picked up by an Allied destroyer.

THE BIRTH OF "LITTLE NORWAY"

in Toronto two months after the temporary defeat in Norway, presented a real problem. Pictured below you see the Technical Chief puzzling over a difficult question in the layout of the first building. The latest addition was two-floored "Radio City".

On the right hand page is "Little Norway" from the air, a completely modern military camp.

"HE CAME THE USUAL WAY..."

remarked the clerk to the recruiting officer, after the new arrival told how he had escaped from Norway and around the world via Russia, Turkey, India, South Africa and South America.

New arrivals show their passports at the camp, report and get military identification cards with photos and fingerprints.

. . . BUT THEY GOT A NEW NORWEGIAN UNIFORM AT "LITTLE NORWAY"

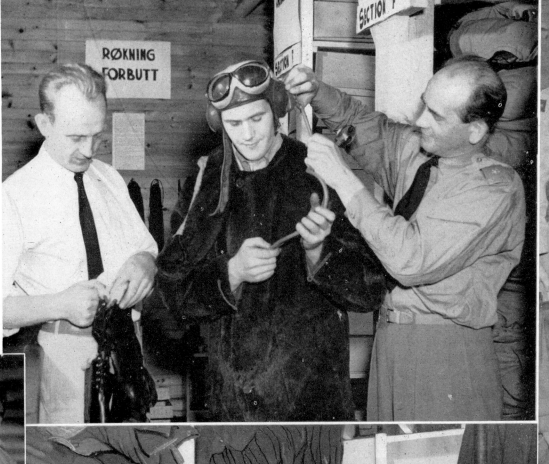

They had to leave their uniforms at home after fighting in Norway and escaped around the world or across the North Sea in civilian clothes to continue the fight. Two of the thousands of volunteers get their new uniforms at the main depot in the camp. They are Norwegian soldiers again! Later on they appear in flying and overseas equipment.

ALMOST AS AT HOME
IN NORWAY . . .

A SOFT AND TOUGH LIFE MIXED WITH SHOOTING . . .

is the recruits' first experience when they train at Lakeside Home—a Paradise for the sons of the summer sun on the shores of Lake Ontario. In the first weeks you must learn to be an all-round and well-disciplined infantry soldier. During this period you have an opportunity—in your daily work—to show your "bosses" what you may be best fitted for afterwards in the various branches of the Air Force.

THEY SYMBOLIZE THE FIGHTING YOUTH FROM NORWAY

Every one of the boys may have an interesting story to tell you about the longest and most dangerous road in history for volunteers. However, the situation makes the man—as the saying goes—and they feel that every young person who can't live without freedom, would have done the same if they had been in their position. If they should happen to tell you their story, it's just to try to convince you of the terrible fate that awaits you and your country if . .

A GUN CAN BE USED FOR EXERCISE TOO.

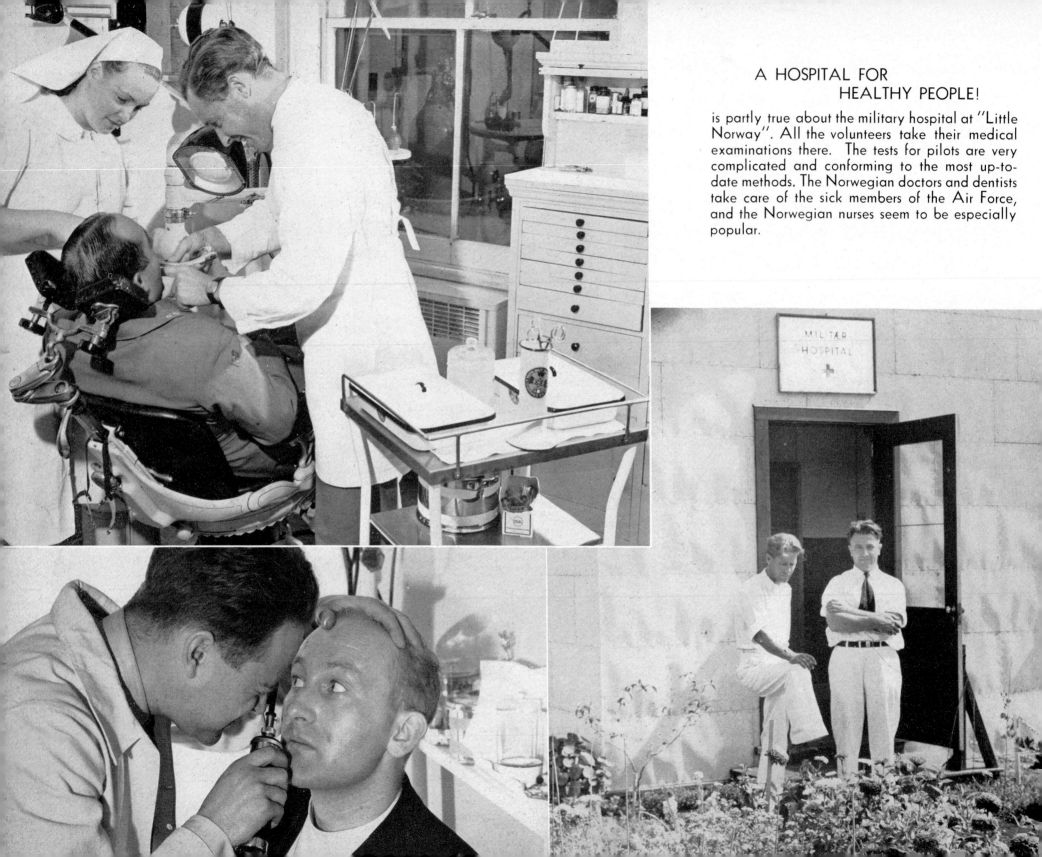

A HOSPITAL FOR HEALTHY PEOPLE!

is partly true about the military hospital at "Little Norway". All the volunteers take their medical examinations there. The tests for pilots are very complicated and conforming to the most up-to-date methods. The Norwegian doctors and dentists take care of the sick members of the Air Force, and the Norwegian nurses seem to be especially popular.

MILITÆR
HOSPITAL

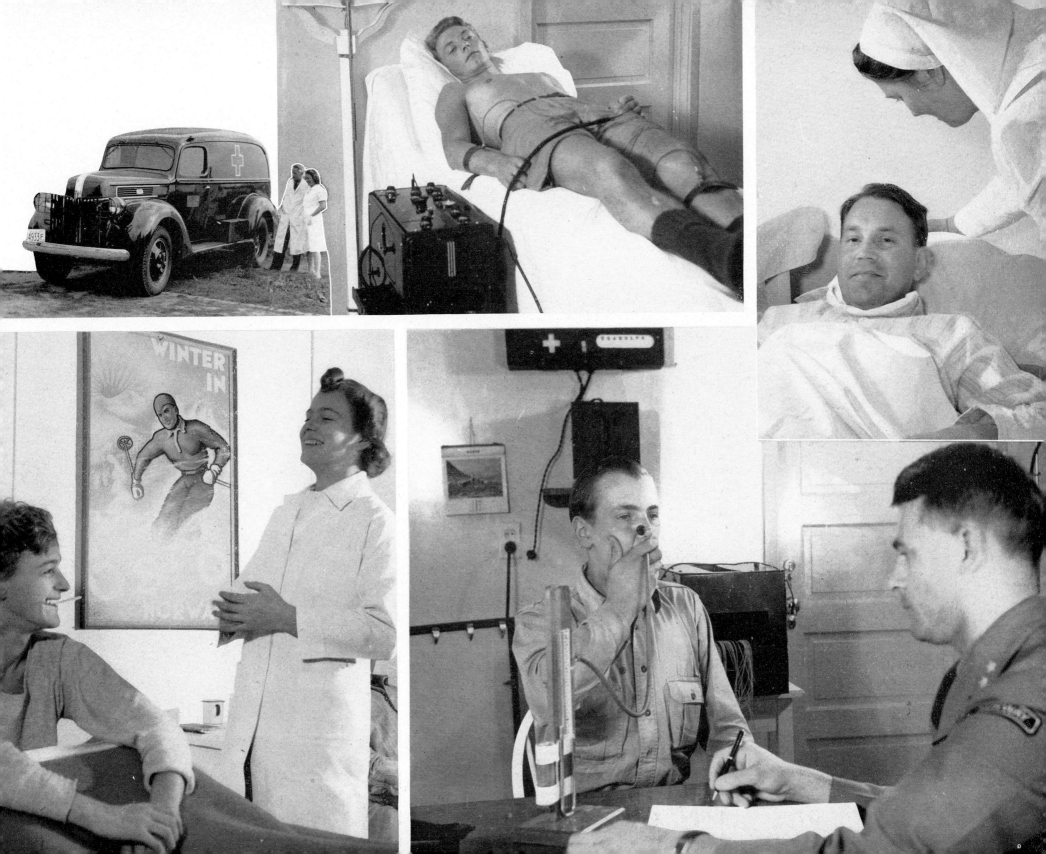

YOU CAN'T ESCAPE FROM TEACHING

A modern Air Force means seventy-five percent technique. War today demands specialists. If you are not, you must study for months to be members of air or ground crews or in one of the many branches that "make and keep you flying."

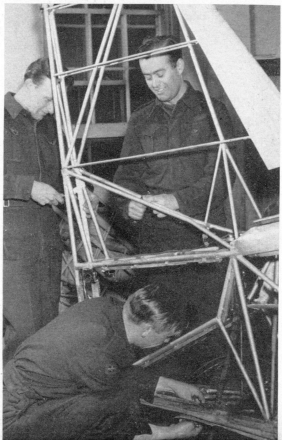

It takes many months to know how . . . . .

THEY DIDN'T REACH NORWAY IN TIME

to be used against Hitler when he suddenly attacked Norway the 9th of April, 1940, on the road to his own destruction. The Norwegian Government bought U.S. combat planes—about 20 million dollars worth—before the war. They were delivered to "Little Norway", making first class training planes for the boys in the re-organized Royal Norwegian Air Forces.

Fairchild trainers, Curtiss fighters, Douglas attack bombers and Northrop patrol bombers—in service summer and winter. The line-up of planes at the aerodrome is a view especially appreciated by new comers . . .

HITLER IS FEELING THE RESULT OF THIS TRAINING EVERY DAY NOW

These boys in training at "Little Norway" belong now to Norwegian squadrons who have been fighting overseas for more than a year.

The small Norwegian Air Force that met hundreds of Hitler's planes on the morning of April 9th in a suicide dogfight, is today back on the battlefronts in modern avenger units.

YOU NEED TECHNICAL KEYMEN
to organize an Air Force.

AND THEY ARRIVED IN DUE TIME AT "LITTLE NORWAY"

from Norway the "hard" and the "easy" way. They assembled the planes, kept them flying and started to teach the newcomers. To organize a modern Air Force from the very beginning and to be familiar with new planes and equipment —in no time—is quite a job.

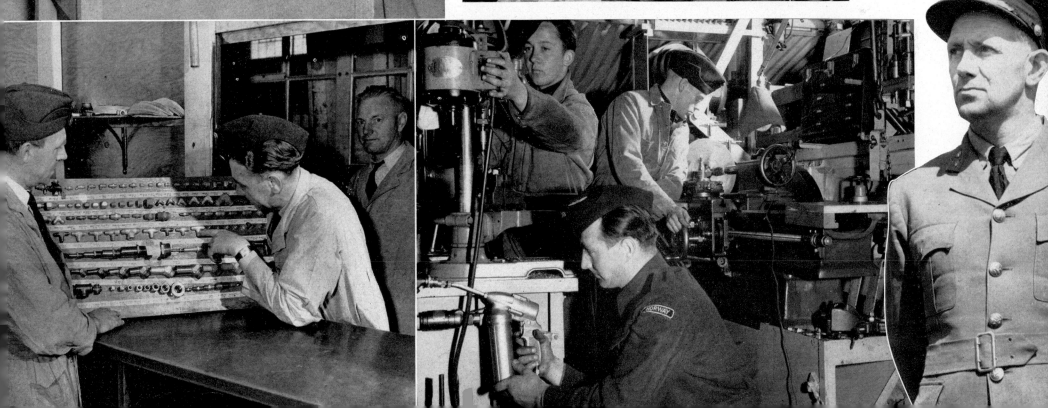

SOME OF THE LEADERS
—and the men in action.

From left to right:—Vice-Admiral Hj. Riiser-Larsen   Lieutenant Colonel B. Oen   Captain Jens S. Hertzberg   Commander A. Hagtvedt

Specialists trained at "Little Norway" lined up for inspection before going overseas.

From left to right:—Major O. B. Engvik   Commander Fr. Vogt   Captain C. F. Jean-Hansen   Major O. Bull

"GOING OVERSEAS"

Crossing many times a day on the peaceful little "Ferry Command" between the camp and the airfield is one of the things that characterizes the daily routine at "Little Norway". In an imperceptible way it may make the boys familiar with the big ferry trip to the fight overseas, on which you see them embarking with a last hearty goodbye to their temporary home—on the road to the final goal of their wishes.

WE ARE ALL RESPONSIBLE...

Do you recognize any of your knitted gifts to the R.N.A.F.? Anyway, the Norwegian women and their Allied friends take care of them so well that a recruit may have a chance to wear the same socks in "Little Norway" and in Norway. They compete peacefully with the shoemaker—the oldest man in camp—and his boys who repair all the shoes to make more holes in the socks . . .

"THE KING IS FEEDING US WELL"

said the Viking in the old Saga, and the boys today agree with him as they enjoy good food—prepared in Norwegian manner—for Norwegian stomachs. The menu for the day is based upon the famous recipes of the "Oslo Breakfast", and other up-to-the-minute discoveries of the "military secrets" in a vitamin-conscious world.

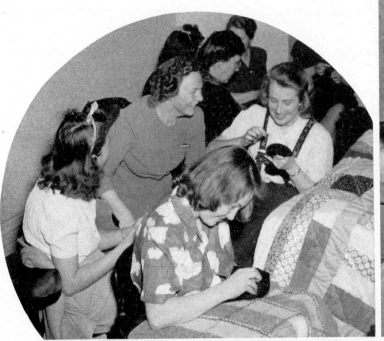

WOULDN'T YOU LIKE TO JOIN THE R.N.A.F.

when you see so many charming girls taking care of the troubles of a bachelor in camp? However, don't think that these girls have time to mend only. This is just "recreation". Women in modern warfare are doing men's work—even in the front line. These girls are busy during the day in hospitals and offices and more girls are wanted by the R.N.A.F. to build up regular units to release men for overseas duty.

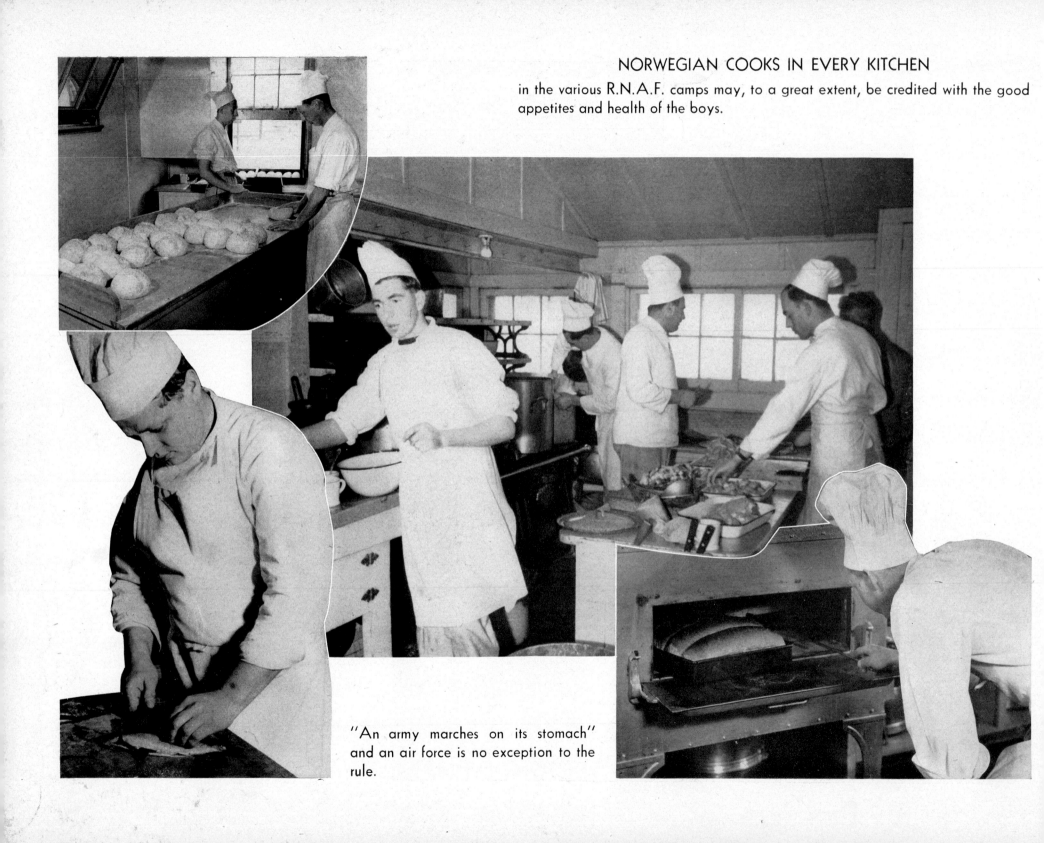

NORWEGIAN COOKS IN EVERY KITCHEN

in the various R.N.A.F. camps may, to a great extent, be credited with the good appetites and health of the boys.

"An army marches on its stomach" and an air force is no exception to the rule.

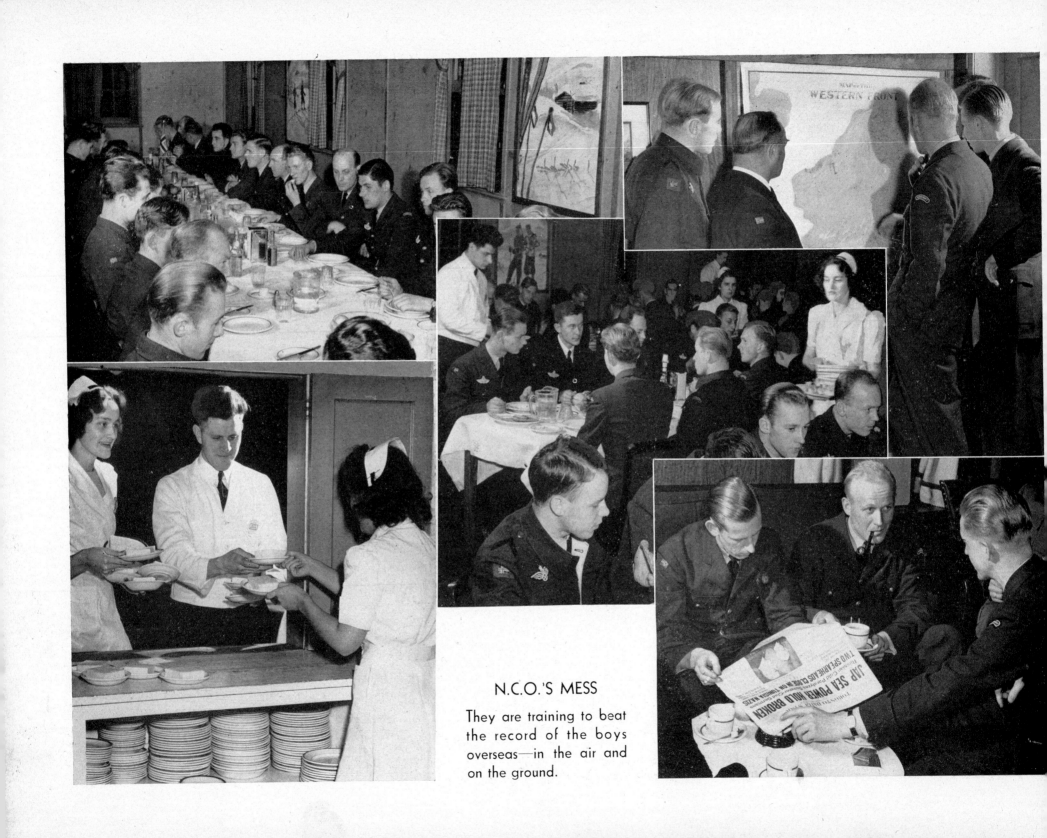

N.C.O.'S MESS

They are training to beat the record of the boys overseas—in the air and on the ground.

SNAPSHOTS FROM THE OFFICERS' MESS AT "LITTLE NORWAY"

Some of them were over Dieppe . . .

WAR IS NOT ALWAYS DESTRUCTION

The peaceful pines around Muskoka Aerodrome are felled and made into log buildings. Norwegian and Finnish-born specialists are carrying out the ideas of the Norwegian architect in building a new training centre for the student pilots.

MUSKOKA AERODROME OPENED BY CROWN PRINCE OLAV ON MAY 4th, 1942.

The log building and the barn—rebuilt for living quarters—characterize the foreign touch . . .

THE FLAG SYMBOLIZES YOUR COUNTRY

Every morning and evening you salute it in honour of your people, its traditions and hopes for the future. It's a part of yourself and your unit. The Norwegian flag bears the insignia of a cross. It indicates that the Norwegian people wish to serve and not to rule. On the homefront today, they prefer to sacrifice their lives rather than change those principles to the "new order". They are the great inspiration to their fighting boys abroad.

THEY WILL LIVE IN THE HISTORY OF NORWAY

SUNSHINE IN THE TRAINING ON THE ROAD TO BERLIN

In the lovely Canadian sunshine at the peaceful aerodrome deep in the woods of Muskoka, pilots study the elementary principles of flying while the ground crew refuel the planes and record the flying hours. Berlin is 3,676 miles away, but they will get there.

MILITARY DISCIPLINE

has to be recognized from the very beginning of training. In action it's vitally important not to ask why . . .

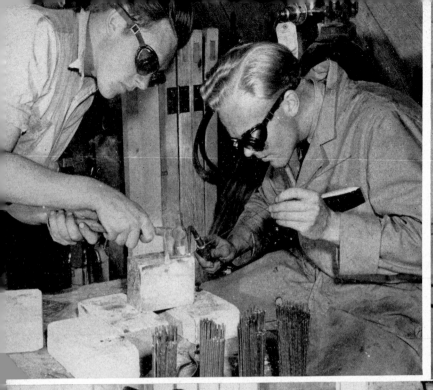

THE ENGINES MUST NOT FAIL . . .

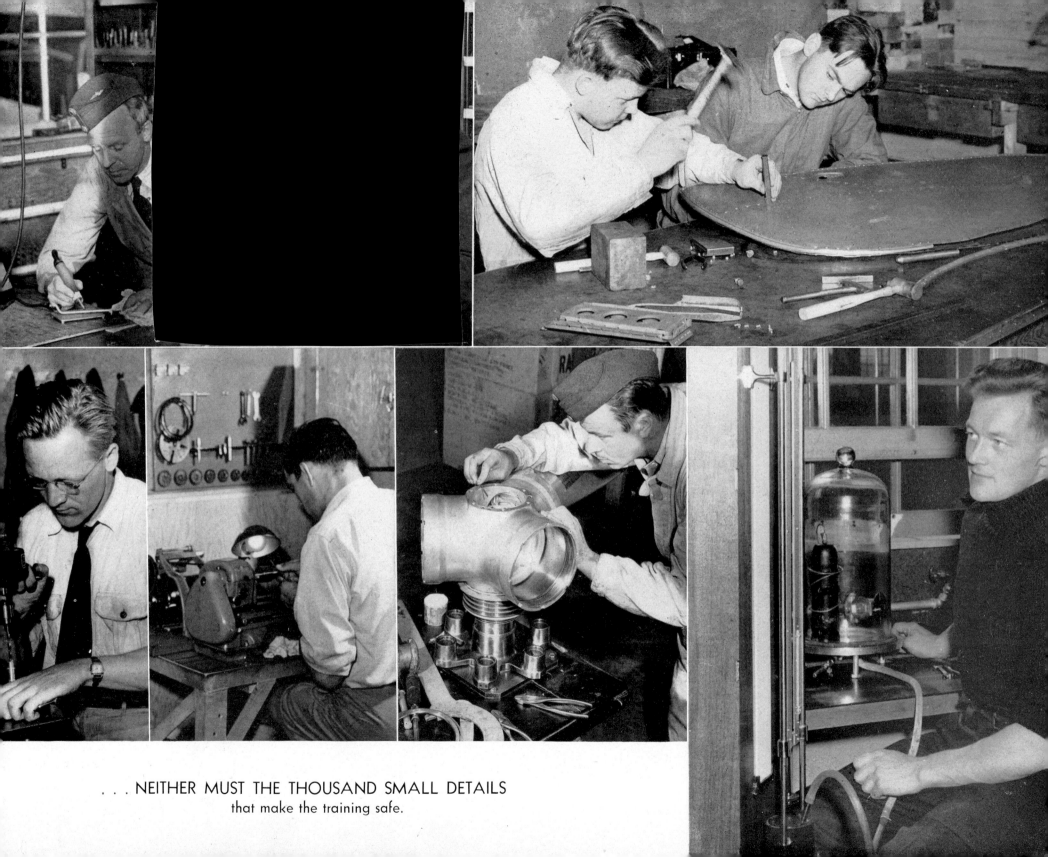

. . . NEITHER MUST THE THOUSAND SMALL DETAILS
that make the training safe.

THE MEN WHO KEEP 'EM FLYING

Maintenance and complete overhaul becomes routine work after a while. But one day you may find a student pilot standing — very depressed — on a farmer's field looking at something that was his plane. However, the experts can fix that too.

WHEN THE PILOT IS SMILING THE SERVICE IS GOOD

He will enjoy the call to duty and handle his plane to the admiration of the newcomers.

THEY ARE COMING DIRECT FROM NORWAY

One of the thousands of "long distance birds" who still has the shadow of the Nazi terror in his eyes after recently escaping over the North Sea. Changing from civilian to soldier, he joins the ranks.

... AND ALL OF THEM WANT TO BE PILOTS

because it's the quickest way to the heart of Berlin.

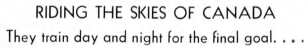

RIDING THE SKIES OF CANADA
They train day and night for the final goal. . . .

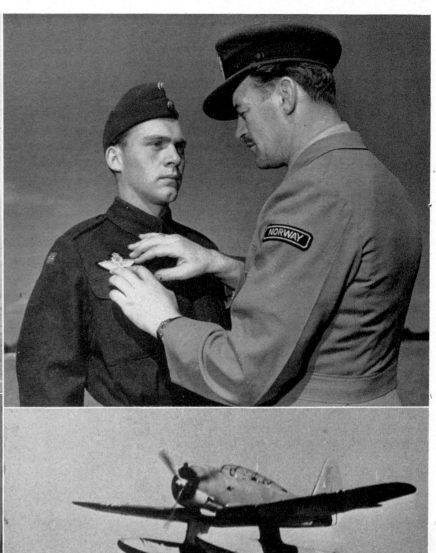

... TO GET THEIR WINGS

and leave for combat duty over enemy territory and the Atlantic, in Norwegian fighter and bomber units.

DEEP IN THE CANADIAN FORES[T]

you can build the ideal home for recreat[ion]
in wartime. Canadian log-building special[ists]
have follow[ed]
the ideas of [a]
Norwegian ar[chi]-
tect so perfe[ctly]
that you can al[most]
"smell" Norwa[y]

"Vesle Skaugum" is this ideal place but it is not for vacation only. Military training is also in progress during the autumn and winter months.

The huskies, under command of "The Major"—are also training for war work in a possible invasion.

"VESLE SKAUGUM"

named after Crown Prince Olav's residence in Norway. The men's canteen fund and gifts from friends bought the place and pay for its upkeep. When the boys, as youngsters in Norway, read Cooper's popular Indian stories, and practised their "wisdom" on chickens and fellow playmates, they didn't dream of the possibility of ever becoming the "Pathfinder" on the famous old warpaths in Canada's forests.

REAL RECREATION

is possible when you are far away from civilization and can disappear deep in the "No Trespassing" property of the bears, beavers, wolves and moose.

THEY ARE IN THE AIR FORCE NOW!

doing their bit in various lo
fights with rats and skunks
ambulance work and the m
peaceful jobs such as enterto
ing. The horse doesn't c
about the gas rationing but
pigs are a little worried ab
Christmas . . . the bear kn
how to bow for a prince.

Canada will always live in the hearts of the Norwegian boys.

COMMANDOS

is a popular word today and the boys take voluntary training when off duty to keep in condition and to learn all the latest tricks. You never know . . . you may have use for them some day. The Commando Units in the Norwegian Army in Scotland have already—as spearheads in the raids on Norway—practised these tricks on the Germans with great success, so the boys know that the tactics really work.

On the page to the right you see various forms of camouflage.

BARRIE 5 M
BRADFORD 27 M
AURORA 38 M
LANGSTAFF 49 M
THORNHILL 51 M
TORONTO 62 M

AIGHURST 8 M
LLSDALE 12 M
R LAKE 16 M
AVERLEY 18 M
IDLAND 27 M
ENETANG 29 M

HIGHWAY Nº 11
ORILLIA 20 M
SEVERN BRIDGE 33 M
GRAVENHURST 45 M

MARCHING 160 MILES IN EIGHT DAYS
after recruit school at "Vesle Skaugum."

ARRIVING AT "LITTLE NORWAY"
still marching with full equipment, and memories of sore feet and friendly civilians.

SWEAT—BUT NO TEARS

in the 21-mile cross-country race with full equipment. Quite a feat—especially in heavy rain. Following an old Norwegian tradition, officers and men compete in a yearly condition test. All agree that a pause on the way under a blanket, a drink of hot soup and bananas, taste like manna from heaven.

YOU CAN FLY WITHOUT WINGS

and the boys never miss an opportunity to do so when off duty. Ola, a student pilot from "Little Norway" and last year's All-American Champion, illustrates a "take-off" and a "Telemark." The boys in the air demonstrate the ultimate in flying style. Our Allies pay them the compliment of being "born with skiis", but sometimes the boys get the impression that their Allied competitors are born in the same way.

IN WINTERTIME AT "VESLE SKAUGUM"

the boys go through the Recruit School—on skiis. However, when they come to the bayonet fighting they have to take off their skiis—even in training. Their good friends, the huskies, are anxious to follow them —straight home to Norway.

ENTENTE CORDIALE
AMONG ALLIES

MUSIC AND CLOSE HARMONY
are sunshine in a camp—sometimes for the listeners too.

He forgot his Accordian

—but he sailed back at night

through mined waters and got it.

EUROPEAN FOOTBALL CAN BE TOUGH TOO

What you haven't in your head you must have in your feet—but hands off the ball.
The boys enjoy competitions with their Allied friends—even when they are beaten.

THE CLASSIC IDEAL OF FIGHTING
is the spirit of ancient Hellas. It gives you good health, good friends and—good luck with the girls.

NORWEGIAN AVIATORS AND SAILORS PARADING ON FIFTH AVENUE
Norwegian-Americans wearing national costumes from the Old Country.

THE 17th
OF
MAY

NORWEGIAN INDEPENDENCE
DAY
—celebrated at "Little Norway"
in the old tradition—with a touch
of Old Canada.

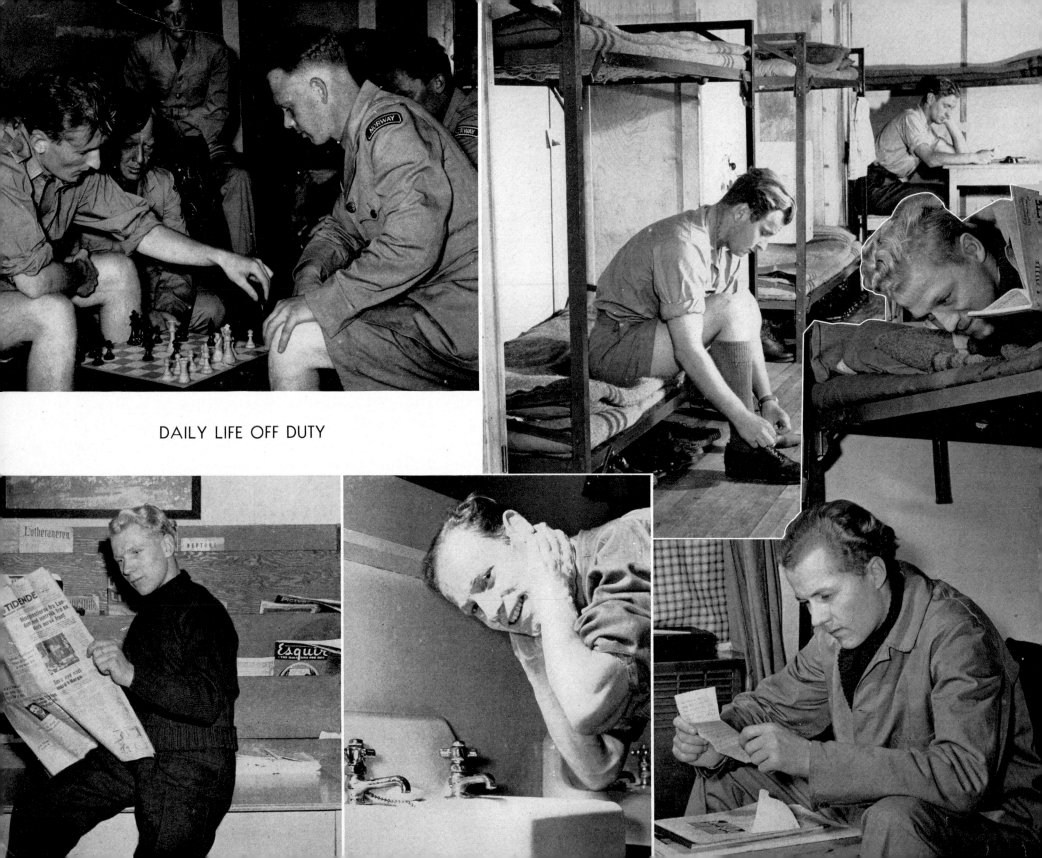

DAILY LIFE OFF DUTY

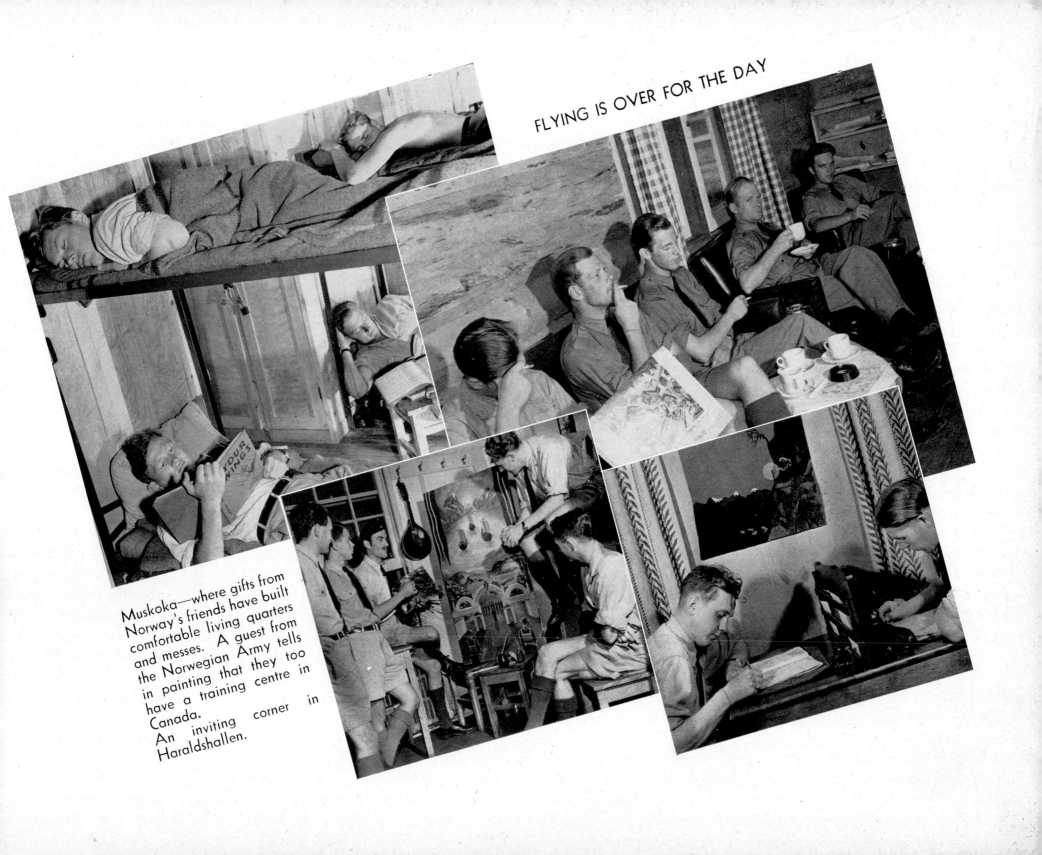

Muskoka—where gifts from Norway's friends have built comfortable living quarters and messes. A guest from the Norwegian Army tells in painting that they too have a training centre in Canada.
An inviting corner in Haraldshallen.

GAVE·FRA·VENNER·AV·NORGE·I·U

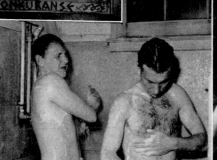

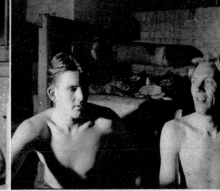

THE BOYS AT "LITTLE NORWAY"

appreciate a gymnasium, Finnish bath and entertainment — it may be a good book, a play, a pretty girl — or an ugly car. The Toronto Sports Service League is their very good friend in all questions of sport — and as far as the girls are concerned they seem to know how to charm the boys.

THE PAST

THE PRESENT

THE FUTURE

A pilot describes the battle at the old Fortress Oscarsborg . . . the escape to England with look-out for Hitler's subs. The voyage continues to Canada where they, after training and friendly associations with Canadians, repay Hitler over Berlin, and return to Norway to the big victory parade in Oslo.

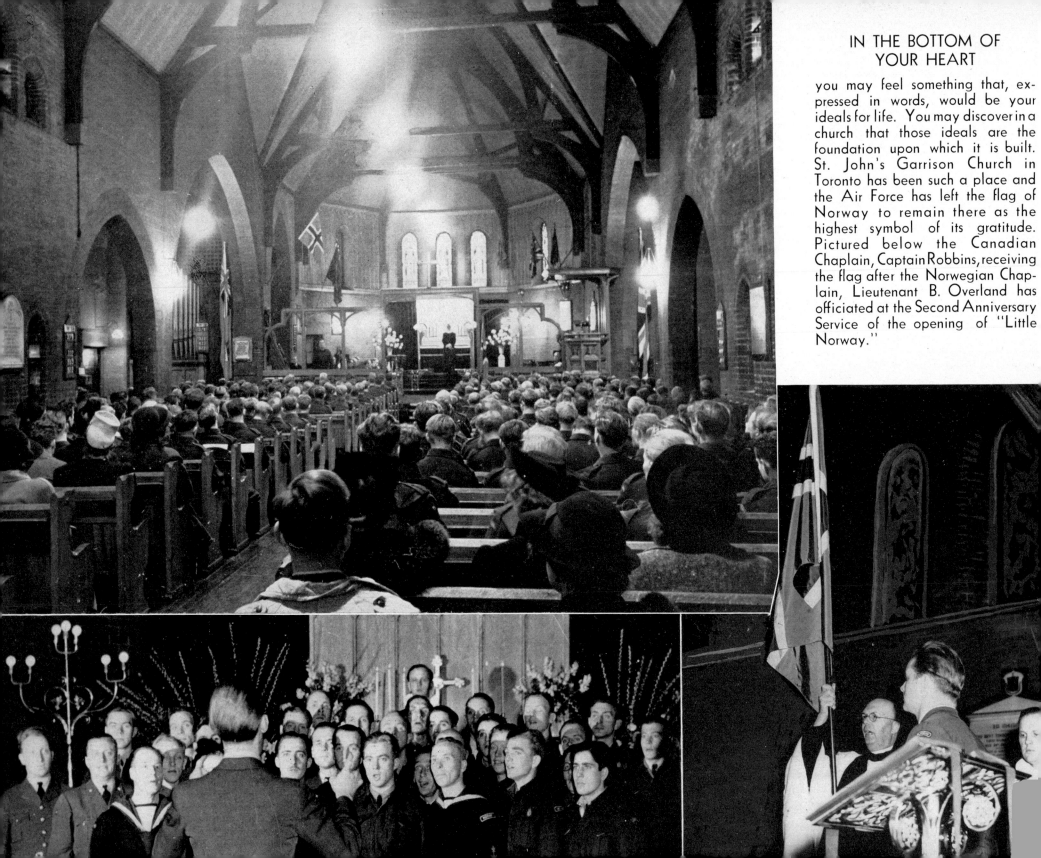

IN THE BOTTOM OF YOUR HEART

you may feel something that, expressed in words, would be your ideals for life. You may discover in a church that those ideals are the foundation upon which it is built. St. John's Garrison Church in Toronto has been such a place and the Air Force has left the flag of Norway to remain there as the highest symbol of its gratitude. Pictured below the Canadian Chaplain, Captain Robbins, receiving the flag after the Norwegian Chaplain, Lieutenant B. Overland has officiated at the Second Anniversary Service of the opening of "Little Norway."

IN HONOUR OF THE BOYS WHO HAVE GIVEN THEIR LIVES.

But their valour is immortal.

THE VISITS OF CROWN PRINCE OLAV AND
CROWN PRINCESS MÄRTHA
have been like a greeting from Norway.

PRINCE HARALD the five-year-old future King of Norway, on his first visit to "Little Norway" with Princesses Ragnhild and Astrid. Being a sweet but tough little King-to-be, he conquered all hearts at once.

He was especially fond of flying in the Link Trainer, christening planes—and bathing in chilly October water.

SALUTING OUR SAILORS

The Norwegian Merchant Marine has supplied Great Britain with 50 per cent of her oil and one-third of her other supplies during the war. Its income pays all the expenses of the Armed Forces in training and action. The Norwegian Navy helps convoy.

Our boys heartily welcomed the representatives of the 25,000 Norwegian sailors who battle on the seven seas. They will also remember the reception by the people of Toronto—especially "Miss Canada."

THE CHRISTMAS CELEBRATION

far from home, separated from your closest relatives and with little information about their fate in an occupied country, contains a certain note of sadness. However, thousands of gifts from friends in North and South America keep the boys smiling.

GOVERNMENT OFFICIALS ON INSPECTION TOURS
Prime Minister J. Nygaardsvold
President of the Parliament J. Hambro
Norwegian Ambassador to the United States, W. Morgenstierne
accompanied by Mr. and Mrs. Anthony Drexel Biddle, American Ambassador to Norway.

Mr. C. Aubrey Smith was an interested visitor.

Air Chief Marshal Sir Frederick Bowhill likes Norwegian pilots in his Ferry Command.

VISITORS TO "LITTLE NORWAY"

H.R.H. the late Duke of Kent and the Mayor of Toronto. Mr. and Mrs. Wendell Willkie. Mrs. J. Borden Harriman, former United States Minister to Norway. Air Vice-Marshall G. E. Brookes. The Norwegian skating star, Miss Erna Andersen.

THE RETURN OF NORSEMEN TO CANADA

has been commemorated by adding a propeller to the collection of Vikings' weapons in the Toronto Museum. Members of the Norwegian Government-in-exile, Messrs. O. Torp, O. Hindahl, N. Hjelmtveit and S. Nielsen inspecting. Air Marshal L.S. Breadner, Canada's Chief-of-the-Air-Staff, with the Norwegian Minister to Canada, Mr. D. Steen at the opening of "Little Norway." The Atlantic flyer, Mr. T. Solberg and Mr. P. Sivertsen with their gift planes to the Air Force.

THE BEST WAY OF HELPING DENMARK

is to assist "Little Norway," said the Danish Minister to the United States, Mr. H. de Kauffmann, when he visited the camp to inspect a number of Danish boys in the R.N.A.F. Crown Princess Märtha with Bernt Balchen and Consul General R. Christensen. The Right Hon. Malcolm MacDonald — High Commissioner to Canada for the United Kingdom, and the Hon. Albert Matthews, Lieutenant Governor of Ontario. To the right is the R.C.A.F. Liaison Officer with the R.N.A.F., Flight Lieutenant S. G. K. MacDonald.

LIKE GULLIVER HIMSELF

the former representative to Canada for the Norwegian Ministry of Defence General W. Steffens, welcomes "El Gaucho" the South American hero— as a mascot of the first gift plane from Argentine and Uruguay. Past and present Norwegian Military Attachés to the United States Lieut.-Col. B. Motzfeld and Commander K. Ostby. General C. G. Fleischer, former C.O. of the Forces in the north of Norway on a visit to the camp. Our two outstanding "reservists," Messrs. Leif Lind Pettersen of Guatemala and Georg Unger Vetlesen of New York, visiting the camp in their voluntary work for the Air Force.

A BOY TOLD HIS STORY

at one of the thousand affairs arranged for the benefit of "Little Norway." The radio and world press publicized it and among the millions who read the story were Donald Crisp, Joe E. Brown, Nancy Carrol and Miss United States Navy. They had to see the camp too. Mr. Louis de Rochemont, Director of The March of Time, almost joined the R.N.A.F. when he made the historic film of Norway's war effort today. The Canadian Broadcasting Corporation has been an especially good friend. The Chiefs of the Norwegian Information Services: Press Attaché S. Oftedal, Montreal; Counsellor Hans Olav, Washington; and Director T. Kandal, New York, discussing public relations in the camp.

THE SWEDISH-AMERICANS DIDN'T FORGET
a Scandinavian friend in his dark days. They collected $100,000 for planes—as a first expression of their feelings.

The United States authorities loaned them an army plane for that purpose —flown from coast to coast by R.N.A.F. boys as a "Message of Goodwill" between Allies. Swedish journalist visiting the camp.

WINGS FOR NORWAY
Fra Norsk-Amerikanere

WINGS FOR NORWAY
Fra Dansk-Amerikanere

WINGS FOR NORWAY
Fra Alberto J. Gundersen & Cia.

FØDSELSDAGSGAVE TIL HAAKON 7
ARGENTINA OG URUGUAY
Argentina og Uruguay

AN INSPIRING PROOF OF THE FEELING FOR NORWAY
among our friends in South America. In North America the "Second Army" is organized mainly by the "Camp Little Norway Association." The boys too, have increased the "Gift Squadron."

THE STAFF AT OUR HEADQUARTERS

In the circle the Air Officer Commanding, Lieut.-Col. Ole Reistad, and at the extreme upper left corner the Chief of Staff, Commander Ole Remlapp.

"LITTLE NORWAY"

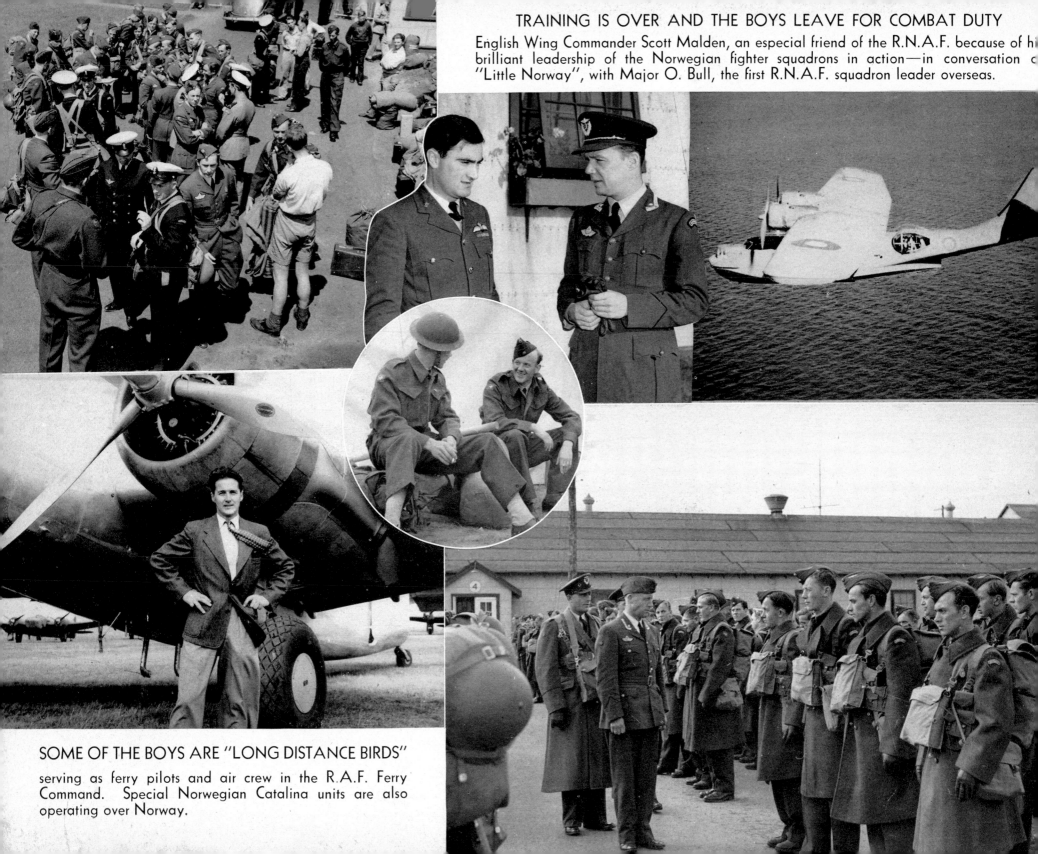

TRAINING IS OVER AND THE BOYS LEAVE FOR COMBAT DUTY

English Wing Commander Scott Malden, an especial friend of the R.N.A.F. because of hi[s] brilliant leadership of the Norwegian fighter squadrons in action—in conversation [at] "Little Norway", with Major O. Bull, the first R.N.A.F. squadron leader overseas.

SOME OF THE BOYS ARE "LONG DISTANCE BIRDS"

serving as ferry pilots and air crew in the R.A.F. Ferry Command. Special Norwegian Catalina units are also operating over Norway.

NORWEGIAN PATROL BOMBERS AT ICELAND

They convoy ships on the Atlantic. German submarines don't like them but the Norwegian and Allied freighters do. The R.A.F. have given them much credit.

NORWEGIAN FIGHTER PILOTS IN SOUTHERN ENGLAND

operating in "All-Norwegian" Spitfire Squadrons, and as pilots in the R.A.F. "Stand by to Attack," and rushing to their planes is daily routine. One of the Avengers from "Little Norway" demonstrates to his comrades how he shot down a Nazi bomber over the channel.

RETURNING FROM THE FIGHT OVER DIEPPE

the Norwegian fighter squadrons were officially credited with one of the highest scores of enemy planes — 16 destroyed and ten damaged — with a loss of two pilots themselves. The R.A.F. awarded the Distinguished Flying Cross to the squadron leaders — one a Dane — and H.M. King Haakon honored them with the Norwegian War Cross. Other pilots were cited for bravery. The boys looking at bullet holes and re-loading the guns. King Haakon, inspiring leader of the Norwegian people today, and the Royal Family, on a visit. The Commanding Officer of the Norwegian Armed Forces, General W. Hansteen, talking with the pilots. The squadron leaders still carrying on after years of fighting.

FREEDOM AND PEACE—FOREVER—IS THE GOAL FOR OUR FIGHT

SOUTHAM PRESS TORONTO
PRINTED IN CANADA